ACID AND BASICS

ACID AND BASICS

A Guide to Understanding Acid–Base Disorders

Jerome Lowenstein, M.D.

Illustrations by
Ronald Markman

"There is something antic about creating, although
the enterprise be serious. And there is a matching
antic spirit that goes with writing about it...

Jerome Bruner
"On Knowing"

New York   Oxford
Oxford University Press
1993

Oxford University Press

Oxford New York Toronto
Delhi Bombay Calcutta Madras Karachi
Kuala Lumpur Singapore Hong Kong Tokyo
Nairobi Dar es Salaam Cape Town
Melbourne Auckland Madrid

and associated companies in
Berlin Ibadan

Published by Oxford University Press, Inc.,
200 Madison Avenue, New York, New York 10016

Oxford is a registered trademark of Oxford University Press

Library of Congress Cataloging-in-Publication Data
Lowenstein, Jerome,
Acid and basics: a guide to understanding acid–base disorders/
text by Jerome Lowenstein; illustrations by Ronald Markman.
p. cm.
Includes bibliographical references and index.
ISBN 0-19-507572-2—ISBN 0-19-507573-0 (pbk.)
1. Acid base imbalances. I. Title.
[DNLM: 1. Acid–Base Equilibrium. 2. Acid–Base Imbalance. WD 220 L917a]
RC630.L68 1993
616.3'9—dc20
DNLM/DLC for Library of Congress 92-16192

9 8 7 6 5 4 3 2 1

Printed in United States of America
on acid-free paper

To my wife, Leahla,
for her love, her support,
and so much more

FOREWORD

Life is an unbelievably delicate proposition. It depends for its existence upon the intricate interrelationship of thousands of different molecules and individual atoms, all of them in constant change, but maintaining a balance.

If we want to be metaphorical, one can view life as a long stick balanced on the nose of a circus performer. It sways back and forth, but the performer's head movements prevent the sway from going too far from the equilibrium position in any direction. As long as the stick remains close enough to equilibrium, it remains "alive." Let it swing in one direction just an inch too far for the performer to compensate and, inexorably, it falls over and "dies."

The life-equilibrium is maintained within the body, despite the fact that conditions outside the body are often far from what the body needs to continue living. The same may be said of cells within the body. One saving grace is that the body is wrapped in skin that protects it from the imbalance of the outer world and cells are bounded by membranes.

The delicate balance of hydrogen ion concentration in cells and in the extracellular fluid which bathes them is maintained within narrow limits, like the balanced stick, by constant adjustments in the transport of protons. The macroscopic elements of acid–base equilibrium, buffering, the production of acids and bases from dietary sources and metabolic processes, and the elimination of acids and bases through the kidney, lung, and gastrointestinal tract have been described by natural scientists for hundreds of years and have been the subject of investigation by physiologists for the past century.

Modern cell and molecular biology provide the conceptual framework and the information to understand acid–base equilibrium and the clinical disorders of acid–base imbalance at a new level, that of membrane ion transport.

With the utmost delicacy, transport proteins facilitate the movement of ions across the cell membranes and preserve acid-base balance. It is this process which Jerome Lowenstein describes in full detail, and starting from scratch in this book. It is impossible to read this book and fail to understand the ins and outs of the process and, moreover, to get an appreciation of the wonders and delicacy of the intricate organization that leads to what we call life.

Isaac Asimov
1991

PREFACE

"Why write a book on the subject of acid–base physiology?" First, I know of no other subject which seems so inaccessible to medical students and young physicians. For me, the challenge to make this subject understandable is akin to the attraction that Mount Everest holds for those who regard themselves as climbers. Second, the past ten years have seen an explosion in knowledge regarding the molecular basis for membrane transport. This information, like earlier advances which clarified the biochemical nature of acids, bases, and buffers, permits an understanding of the physiologic basis for acid–base disorders at a level not previously possible.

This "guide" is an attempt to lead the uninitiated and the timid to an understanding of acid–base disorders. I recognize that this tour will not include all the disorders of acid–base physiology; this was a conscious choice made with the hope of developing a conceptual framework rather than a reference source.

I am indebted to many of my colleagues for the years of challenging conferences and discussions which have greatly influenced my understanding of acid–base disorders. I owe even more to countless medical students whose questions forced me to examine my own knowledge.

Special acknowledgement must be given to Dr. Jose Zadunaisky who opened my mind to the importance of membrane ion transport and invited me to work with him at the Mt. Desert Island Biological Laboratory. This book has its roots in that extraordinary intellectual environment on the coast of Maine.

The rigorous criticism and comments of Drs. David Goldfarb, Pierre Dagher, Alan Charney and Kotresha Neelakantappa and long discussions with these outstanding colleagues were important in clarifying or formulating many of the ideas contained in the book. I am very grateful to Dr. Gerald Weissmann for his generous support and his valuable advice through the development of this idea. The help and encouragement of Dr. David S. Baldwin, Dr. Will Grossman, and my friend, Serge Sabarsky, is gratefully acknowledged. Lynn Leung, Amy Wallace, and Celia Harkins typed the endless revisions of the text. Sui Leong was a tireless proofreader.

I am especially indebted to Kirk Jensen of Oxford University Press for recognizing my intent and encouraging me to pursue the "difficult balancing act" represented in this book. His fine sense of style and wise counsel are very much appreciated.

Finally, I am deeply indebted to Ronald Markman for creating a set of illustrations which have captured the spirit in which the book was written. Ronald Markman is Professor of Fine Arts at Indiana University. His paintings and prints are included in many public collections including the murals for the Riley Children's Hospital in Indianapolis.

New York   J. L.
April 1992

CONTENTS

ACID AND BASICS

A Brief Historical Overview: To Abstract Concept and Back Again

The concepts of *acidity* and *alkalinity*, based on direct sensory experience, were well known in the biblical period although the chemical composition of acids and alkali was virtually unknown, and would remain so until well into the nineteenth century. Acids were identified as substances which tasted sour (Latin, *acere* = sour). The prototypic acid, acetic acid, was a product of the fermentation of grapes. Acids were also known to have the properties of etching some metals and certain soft stones and of producing a color change in some dyestuffs, such as litmus. Alkalis were identified as substances, produced by the burning of some plants, which had the property of neutralizing or blocking the actions of acids. The word alkali is derived from the Arabic *al-qily* meaning "to roast in a pan" or "the calcined ashes of plants." "Acid" and "alkali" were familiar to most people through everyday experience, much as "gravity" is experienced in day-to-day living.

The prescientific concept of acids and bases was carried, without substantive modification, through the Middle Ages and on up to the early nineteenth century. A school of medicine, iatrochemistry (literally, medical chemistry), which ascribed a role to various acids and alkali in the causation of disease, flourished in the sixteenth and seventeenth centuries. In the nineteenth and early twentieth century, with careful observations and the development of instruments for measuring acid in biologic fluids, acidosis was identified as an important clinical feature of Asiatic cholera and diabetic coma. Physiologists at the beginning of the twentieth century explored acid balance in animals and in man, utilizing measurements of titratable acid in urine and newly developed methods for measuring carbon dioxide in blood. These carefully documented observations led to the formulation of many of the principles which are central to our present-day understanding of acid–base physiology.

The major contributions of physiologists such as Kussmaul, Naunyn, Magnus–Levy, and Lawrence Henderson are all the more remarkable as they antedated fundamental discoveries related to the chemical nature of acids and bases. It was not until the early nineteenth century that the property of acidity was identified with the hydrogen ion. The concept of electrolytic dissociation, first proposed by Svante Arrhenius in 1884, provided the theoretic foundation for the development of the concepts of dynamic equilibrium in solutions and buffering. The modern concept of acids as substances which can *donate* a proton (hydrogen ion) and bases as substances which can *combine with or accept* a proton was formulated by Johannes Brønsted in 1923, but did not attain wide acceptance in medicine and physiology until the 1950s.

The direct sensory-based concept of acids and bases was replaced by a far more abstract concept which, while scientifically far more advanced, could not be perceived directly by the senses and was therefore more difficult to understand. Writing in "The Origin of Consciousness in the Breakdown of the Bicameral Mind" Julian James states, "Understanding a thing is to arrive at a metaphor for that thing by substituting something more familiar to us. And the feeling of familiarity is the feeling of understanding." The modern view of matter as having both the properties of a wave and a particle makes it difficult to cling to the "metaphors" we have employed which "picture" the formation of hydrogen ions as the jumping of electrons from one set of balls and rings to another.

These developments in chemistry and physics, while leaving us with a more abstract concept of acids and bases, provided the foundation for studies of acid and electrolyte transport utilizing kinetic and biophysical methods. The *characteristics* of many transport processes were elucidated before the current era of molecular biology provided a description of the *machinery*, the transport proteins, exchangers, and ion channels. No wonder that acid–base physiology has often been viewed as the arcane province of a few "medical-chemists"!

The past twenty years have been marked by an explosion of information in transport physiology. Much of the new information bears directly on the transport of acids and bases across cell membranes. An understanding of the behavior of transport proteins, derived in many cases from the study of cloned genes and their products, has led to deductions about the structure of the transporters. In many instances these deductions have been confirmed by electron microscopic or crystallographic methods, which give a "picture" of the transport protein.

This book is written with the conviction that this new, albeit "high-tech," sensory-based view of acid transport makes acid–base physiology and disorders of acid–base homeostasis more comprehensible.

... of Water, Hydrogen, Hydrogen Ion, and pH

To understand acid–base disorders we must first spend some time learning about the hydrogen ion, which is the "main player" in this story. Then we will make an excursion into the field of transport physiology.

Hydrogen is the most abundant atom in all cells. Most of the hydrogen is in the form of water. The water molecule has a number of qualities which make it uniquely suited to support life. The high heat capacity of water accounts for the ability of bodies of water to act as "heat reservoirs" and minimizes water loss by evaporation. The expansion of water which occurs as water freezes causes ice to be lighter than water and to float, providing insulation of the underlying water. Water is an excellent solvent for electrolytes and many polar organic molecules. These properties are attributable to the polarity of the water molecule.

In the water molecule (H_2O) the oxygen atom is bound to each of the hydrogen atoms by *covalent bonds* to form an asymmetric molecule. The electrons of the hydrogen atom are drawn toward the oxygen atom creating a polarity (dipole) with a local *positive* charge associated with the hydrogen atoms and local *negative* charge associated with the oxygen atom. Each water molecule behaves like a small magnet with positive and negative poles, resulting in an electrostatic attraction between the hydrogen atom of one water molecule and the oxygen atom of a nearby water molecule. This interaction is referred to as a *hydrogen bond*. This bond, which accounts for many of the physical characteristics of water, is relatively weak compared to the covalent bond between hydrogen and oxygen in the water molecule but is stronger than the intermolecular attraction, van der Waals forces, between nonpolar organic molecules. The "strength" of a bond is measured as the energy (e.g., heat) required to break the bond. The hydrogen bonds between water molecules have a bond energy (strength) of 1 to 2 kcal/mol as compared with 110 kcal/mol for the covalent H—O bond.

There is a tendency for a hydrogen ion to "break loose" from a water molecule and "jump" to the oxygen of adjacent water molecules to which it is hydrogen bonded. Because of the attraction created by the greater mass of the oxygen atom, the single electron donated by the hydrogen atom is "left behind." This dissociation or ionization yields a hydronium ion and a hydroxyl ion. For convenience we usually refer to the products of dissociation of water as *hydroxyl* and *hydrogen* ions and write the equation as

$$H_2O \rightarrow H^+ + OH^-$$

but more correctly, it should be

$$2H_2O \rightarrow H_3O^+ + OH^- \qquad (H_3O^+ \text{ is a hydronium ion})$$

Both the hydroxyl ion and the hydronium ion are attracted to other water molecules by hydrogen bonds. Molecules of water are constantly dissociating to form H^+ and OH^-,

$$H_2O \rightarrow H^+ + OH^-$$

and hydrogen and hydroxyl ions are constantly colliding and associating to form H_2O,

$$H^+ + OH^- \rightarrow H_2O$$

At equilibrium, only a minute fraction of water molecules are ionized. The equation which is used to describe the dissociation of water is:

$$K_{eq} = \frac{[H^+] \times [OH^-]}{[H_2O]}$$

where $[H^+]$, $[OH^-]$, and $[H_2O]$ are the molar concentrations of hydrogen ion, hydroxyl ion, and water. We can use this relationship to estimate the concentration of hydrogen (or hydronium) ions. The equilibrium equation can be arranged to read

$$K_{eq} \times [H_2O] = [H^+] \times [OH^-]$$

The likelihood of collision between H^+ and OH^- increases with an increase in the concentration of either H^+ or OH^-. The expression $K_{eq}[H_2O]$, the "ion product for water," represents the product of the concentrations of H^+ and OH^- at equilibrium. The ion product for water at 25°C is $1 \times 10^{-14} M$. In pure water $[H^+] = [OH^-] = 1 \times 10^{-7} M$ and neutral pH, the negative log of $[H^-] = 7$.

In pure water, at 25°C, the concentration of hydrogen ions is $1 \times 10^{-7} M$ or only 2/1,000,000,000 of the concentration of H_2O molecules. Though H^+ constitutes a very small fraction of the total water, $10^{-7} M$ of H^+ still represents a very large number of ions since a mole of H^+ contains 6.02×10^{23} hydrogen ions.

The concentrations of hydrogen ion and hydroxyl ion are inversely related in aqueous solution. If we add H^+, in the form of a weak or a strong acid, hydrogen ions combine with hydroxyl ions until a new equilibrium is established with a higher $[H^+]$ and lower $[OH^-]$. If the hydrogen ion concentration is increased to $1 \times 10^{-6} M$, the hydroxyl ion concentration will decrease to $10^{-8} M$ (pH = 6).

The hydrogen ion concentration in aqueous solutions varies widely. The pH of drinking water is usually about 5 (i.e., a H^+ concentration of $1 \times 10^{-5} M$). The pH of Coca Cola (before it "goes flat") is 2.8; milk has a pH approximately 6.6. Water in a freshwater pond or fish tank has a pH between 6.8 and 7.2 but marine fish live best at the pH of ocean water, about 8. The pH of body secretions also can vary widely. The most extreme examples are gastric fluid which may have a pH as low as 1.5 ($1 \times 10^{-1.5} M$ H^+) and pancreatic juice which usually has a pH about 8.

In contrast to this wide variation in hydrogen ion concentration in fluids all around us, those that we ingest and those that our body secrete, the concentration of hydrogen ion in the fluid bathing cells in multi-cellular organisms, the extracellular fluid, is maintained within a very narrow range—pH 7.35 to 7.45—representing a hydrogen ion concentration between 45 and 35 nmol/L.

Why is hydrogen ion concentration maintained within such a narrow range?

3

Why Is pH Important in Biologic Systems?

Many other ions in intracellular and extracellular fluids are far more abundant than hydrogen ion. What makes the concentration of hydrogen ion so important in living organisms?

To understand this we have to look at the composition of organic molecules. Organic molecules are composed almost entirely of only a limited number of atoms (see Figure 1).

Organic molecules have a structure consisting of a carbon "backbone"

Straight chain   C—C—C—C—C—

Branched chain
$$C-C-\underset{\underset{C-C}{|}}{\overset{\overset{C-C}{|}}{C}}-C$$

Ring

$$
\begin{array}{c}
C{=}C \\
\diagup \qquad \diagdown \\
C \qquad\quad C \\
\diagdown \qquad \diagup \\
C{-}C
\end{array}
$$

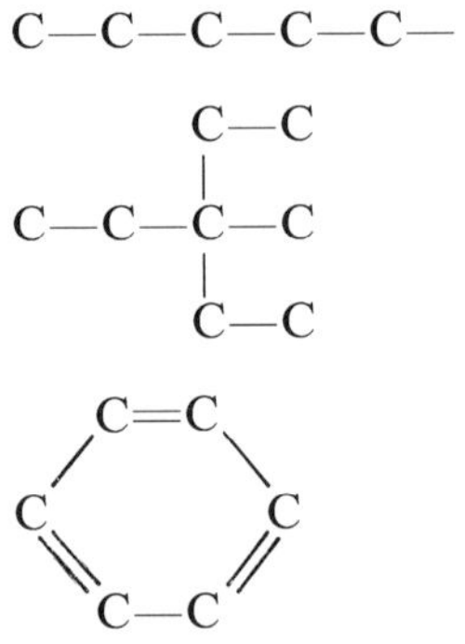

Carbon–carbon bonds are covalent bonds. Electrons in the outer ring of each carbon atom are shared. These bonds have a high energy (83 kcal/mol) and are very stable. Covalent bonds between carbon, oxygen, hydrogen, nitrogen, phosphorus, and sulfur have energies ranging from 50 to 110 kcal/mol.

Periodic Table of the Elements

IA	IIA	IIIB	IVB	VB	VIB	VIIB	VIII			IB	IIB	IIIA	IVA	VA	VIA	VIIA	INERT GASES VIIIA
1 1.00794 *H* Hydrogen																	2 4.002602 *He* Helium
3 6.941 *Li* Lithium	4 9.01218 *Be* Beryllium											5 10.811 *B* Boron	6 12.011 *C* Carbon	7 14.00674 *N* Nitrogen	8 15.9994 *O* Oxygen	9 18.998403 *F* Flourine	10 20.1797 *Ne* Neon
11 22.989768 *Na* Sodium	12 24.3050 *Mg* Magnesium											13 26.981539 *Al* Aluminum	14 28.0855 *Si* Silicon	15 30.973762 *P* Phosphorus	16 32.066 *S* Sulfur	17 35.4527 *Cl* Chlorine	18 39.948 *Ar* Argon
19 39.0983 *K* Potassium	20 40.078 *Ca* Calcium	21 44.95591 *Sc* Scandium	22 47.88 *Ti* Titanium	23 50.9415 *V* Vanadium	24 51.9961 *Cr* Chromium	25 54.93805 *Mn* Manganese	26 55.847 *Fe* Iron	27 58.93320 *Co* Cobalt	28 58.69 *Ni* Nickel	29 63.546 *Cu* Copper	30 65.39 *Zn* Zinc	31 69.723 *Ga* Gallium	32 72.61 *Ge* Germanium	33 74.92159 *As* Arsenic	34 78.96 *Se* Selenium	35 79.904 *Br* Bromine	36 83.80 *Kr* Krypton
37 85.4678 *Rb* Rubidium	38 87.62 *Sr* Strontium	39 88.90585 *Y* Yttrium	40 91.224 *Zr* Zirconium	41 92.90638 *Nb* Niobium	42 95.94 *Mo* Molybdenum	43 98.9063 *Tc* Technetium	44 101.07 *Ru* Ruthenium	45 102.90550 *Rh* Rhodium	46 106.42 *Pd* Palladium	47 107.8682 *Ag* Silver	48 112.411 *Cd* Cadmium	49 114.82 *In* Indium	50 118.710 *Sn* Tin	51 121.75 *Sb* Antimony	52 127.60 *Te* Tellurium	53 126.90447 *I* Iodine	54 131.29 *Xe* Xenon
55 132.90543 *Cs* Cesium	56 137.327 *Ba* Barium	57-71 *La-Lu*	72 178.49 *Hf* Hafnium	73 180.9479 *Ta* Tantalum	74 183.85 *W* Tungsten	75 186.207 *Re* Rhenium	76 190.2 *Os* Osmium	77 192.22 *Ir* Iridium	78 195.08 *Pt* Platinum	79 196.96654 *Au* Gold	80 200.59 *Hg* Mercury	81 204.3833 *Tl* Thallium	82 207.2 *Pb* Lead	83 208.98037 *Bi* Bismuth	84 208.9824 *Po* Polonium	85 209.9871 *At* Astatine	86 222.0176 *Rn* Radon
87 223.0197 *Fr* Francium	88 226.0254 *Ra* Radium	89-103 *Ac-Lr*	104 261.1087 *Unq* Unnilquadium	105 262.1138 *Unp* Unnilpentium	106 263.1182 *Unh* Unnilhexium	107 262.1229 *Uns* Unnilseptium	108 *Uno*	109 *Une*									

57 138.9055 *La* Lanthanum	58 140.115 *Ce* Cerium	59 140.90765 *Pr* Praseodymium	60 144.24 *Nd* Neodymium	61 145.9151 *Pm* Promethium	62 150.36 *Sm* Samarium	63 151.965 *Eu* Europium	64 157.25 *Gd* Gadolinium	65 158.92534 *Tb* Terbium	66 162.50 *Dy* Dysprosium	67 164.93032 *Ho* Holmium	68 167.26 *Er* Erbium	69 168.93421 *Tm* Thulium	70 173.04 *Yb* Ytterbium	71 174.967 *Lu* Lutetium
89 227.0278 *Ac* Actinium	90 232.0381 *Th* Thorium	91 231.0359 *Pa* Protactinium	92 238.0289 *U* Uranium	93 237.0482 *Np* Neptunium	94 244.0642 *Pu* Plutonium	95 243.0614 *Am* Americium	96 247.0703 *Cm* Curium	97 247.0703 *Bk* Berkelium	98 251.0796 *Cf* Californium	99 252.0829 *Es* Einsteinium	100 257.0951 *Fm* Fermium	101 258.0986 *Md* Mendelevium	102 259.1009 *No* Nobelium	103 260.1053 *Lr* Lawrencium

Fig. 1. Carbon, oxygen, nitrogen, hydrogen, phosphorus, and sulfur are the predominant atoms of organic molecules.

Large biologically important molecules, such as proteins, nucleic acids, starches and complex lipids, consist of a series of smaller components (amino acids, sugars, or fatty acids) linked together by covalent bonds formed when a hydroxyl ion of one group and a hydrogen ion of another are removed (forming H_2O) as in these examples:

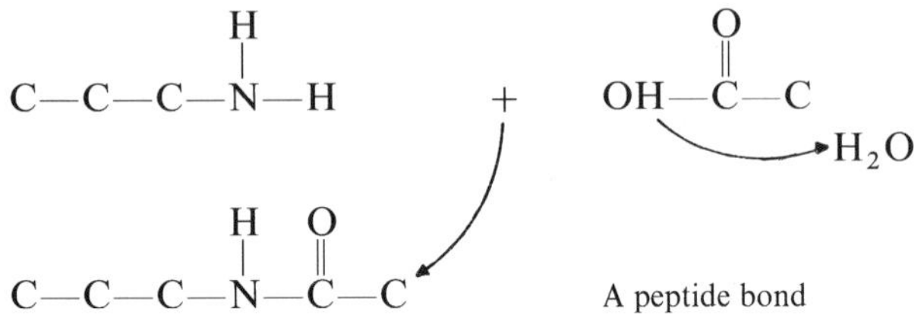

A peptide bond

or

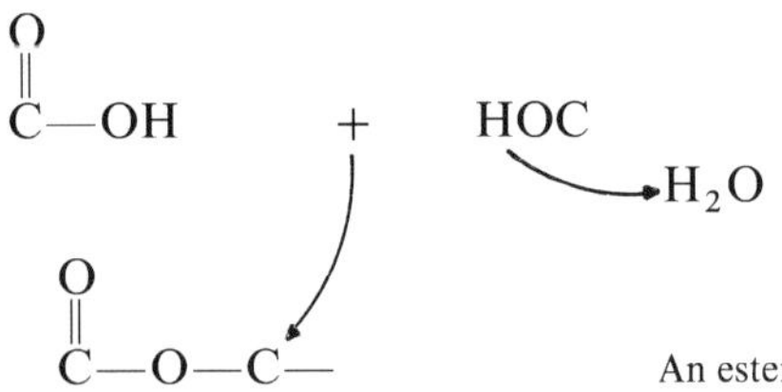

An ester bond

These strong covalent bonds determine the sequence of atoms or the primary structure of large molecules. Large molecules also have shape; some are long and "fibrillar" such as collagen, others such as hemoglobin are round or globular, and some assume very intricate shapes such as the helix that characterizes DNA.

The "shape" of a large molecule such as a protein is determined, in large part, by the amino acid sequence (the primary structure) since peptide bonds and carbon–carbon bonds have restricted bonding angles. Attraction or repulsion between positive- and negative-charged side groups or regions which are more or less hydrophobic yield a molecule with unique secondary (beta-pleated or helix) and tertiary (folding) structure.

Folding such that hydrophobic segments are deep within the molecule (out of contact with the aqueous environment) appears to play a major role in determining the secondary and tertiary structure of large organic molecules. This shape is stabilized by hydrogen bonds between adjacent peptide or other side groups.

Since the dissociation of hydrogen ions from amino acids and other functional groups requires less energy than the disruption of covalent bonds, the hydrogen ion comes to play a role in determining whether a molecule—or a part of a molecule—will have an electric charge and this, in turn, is a determinant of the shape of the molecule and of the attraction or repulsion between parts of a molecule or among molecules within a larger structure (e.g., the cell membrane). It is, therefore, not surprising to find that hydrogen ion concentration effects many functions of large molecules.

Just as the hydrogen ion dissociates and is in equilibrium with the water molecule in solution, so the hydrogen ions of amino acids can be dissociated to form ionic groups. At physiologic pH most of the carboxyl ($-COO^-$) groups of amino acids are completely ionized and the amino ($-NH_2$) groups completely nonionized. The ionization of some side chains, such as the imidazole group of histidine, does vary considerably within the physiologic pH range. This means that when the hydrogen ion concentration of the solution changes, the shape of molecules in that solution changes. The consequences of these shape changes are evident in many different ways. Consider a colored material, a dye, which is an organic molecule of the kind we have been considering. If we add an acid—any acid will do—litmus turns from blue to pink or nitrazine turns by steps through a whole series of colors (reversibly) as the hydrogen ion concentration changes. Other molecules change their fluorescence when [H^+] changes. These changes in color or fluorescence are due to changes in the *shape* of the molecule as hydrogen ions associate or dissociate from the molecule.

There are other properties of molecules which change as a result of alteration in shape brought about by change in H^+ concentration. The catalytic action of enzymes requires that a portion of the enzyme protein and the substrate "fit" together to allow a chemical reaction to occur. The close approximation of enzyme and substrate allows weak attractant forces (van der Waals and hydrophobic interactions) to act. When the [H^+] of the medium changes, the rate of the catalyzed reaction is affected, probably by alterations in these weak attractant forces. Enzymes typically exhibit changes in their activity with varying pH and maximal enzymatic activity is observed over a relatively narrow pH range.

Antigen-antibody reactions, another form of protein–protein interaction, are often pH-dependent.

Ion channels, particularly K^+ channels, exhibit pH-dependence.

The affinity of hemoglobin for oxygen is pH-dependent. This is probably attributable to buffering of H^+ by the abundant histidine residues of hemoglobin.

Factors which control gene transcription and translation may be critically $[H^+]$ dependent. The synthesis of DNA and RNA increase with increasing intracellular pH.

Growth-promoting factors may initiate growth by altering the existing H^+ concentration.

The intracellular "traffic" of proteins, appears to be critically dependent on the pH in subcellular organelles, probably mediated by the modification of protein–protein interactions.

Events in the fertilized ovum appear to be triggered by changes in intracellular pH. Within 1 minute following fertilization, the cytoplasmic pH of the sea urchin egg increases from 6.6 to 7.2 and it is believed by some that this decrease in $[H^+]$ triggers growth and cell division.

Most of the effects of pH which we have been considering are mediated through the interaction of hydrogen ions and intracellular proteins. Let's look at how intracellular hydrogen ion concentration is regulated.

4

The Cell Membrane and Transport Proteins

First we must recognize that the concentrations of the hydrogen ion and all other electrolytes within the cell differ considerably from the concentrations in the bathing medium. Cells are bounded by membranes. These cell membranes are composed of phospholipids and proteins arranged in a very unique manner. Consider the structure of a phospholipid molecule such as phosphatidyl choline which makes up a large part of the cell membrane.

Phosphatidyl Choline

This phosphotriglyceride consists of two long fatty acids and one molecule of phosphoric acid (which is itself esterified with choline) esterified with glycerol. The phosphate group has an electric charge and would be expected to be attracted to the polar solvent, water, that is, it is hydrophilic. The long-chain fatty acids are nonpolar and would be repelled by a polar solvent such as water, that is, they are hydrophobic. When a nonpolar lipid is dispersed in a watery medium, it tends to form droplets. When molecules, such as phospholipids, are dispersed in aqueous media, a "lipid bilayer" is formed. This structure orients nonpolar lipid portions of phospholipids to interact while the polar portions of the molecule interact with the aqueous (polar) external or internal compartments. The lipid droplets formed by molecules such as phospholipids are called micelles or liposomes. In 1935 H. A. Davson and J. F. Danielli proposed that biologic membranes were made up of lipid bilayers.

Protein molecules are incorporated in the lipid bilayer of the cell membrane. Like phospholipids, proteins also have more lipid-soluble ("lipophilic" or "hydrophobic") and more water-soluble ("hydrophilic") portions. In the plasma membrane or lipid bilayer, lipophilic portions of the protein molecule are "attracted" by hydrophobic interactions and tend to cluster together in the lipid inner core of the membrane while the hydrophilic portions of the protein molecule are oriented toward the aqueous medium at the outer or inner interface. These hydrophobic and hydrophilic interactions determine the spatial orientation of proteins which are inserted in the plasma membrane, much as iron filings are oriented by a magnetic field.

The fluid mosaic model of biologic membrane structure proposed by S. J. Singer and G. L. Nicholson in 1972 has been described as a "lipid bilayer containing iceberg-like protein macromolecules spanning the bilayer." While that may seem to be quite a feat of cellular engineering, highly organized membranes such as these can be made simply by homogenizing lipids, protein, and a watery solvent under certain conditions. In fact, there is not much difference between the procedure of making mayonnaise and the process of making "vesicles" or "liposomes," small lipid bilayer-bounded particles which are used as experimental models for cells or cell organelles (Fig. 2).

HOMEMADE MAYONNAISE (according to Craig Claiborne)	HOMEMADE LIPOSOMES (according to Gerald Weissmann, MD)
Ingredients:	Ingredients:
3 egg yolks (lecithin)	75 parts egg yolks (ovolecithin)
2 cups of oil (olive and salad)	10 parts egg yolks (cholesterol)
a dash of vinegar (acetic acid)	15 parts diacetylphosphate (phosphoric acid)

Since the "inner core" of the lipid bilayer is nonpolar, it does not permit the diffusion of small charged ions or molecules across the cell membrane, either into or out of the cell. It serves as a diffusion barrier for polar or charged particles (ions or molecules) and allows for concentration differences between the cytoplasm of the cell and the fluid which bathes it.

Harold Morowitz, writing in "Mayonnaise and the Origin of Life." said,

> From a humanistic point of view, individuality entered the world when the first membrane fragment wrapped itself into a closed shell and separated the interior components from the rest of the universe.

Nonpolar, noncharged molecules can cross these cell membranes fairly readily. This permits oxygen to enter cells and carbon dioxide to leave cells, and permits some very lipid-soluble substances to cross easily into cells, passing directly through the bilayer. The situation is more complex when we deal with ions or polar molecules. The lipid bilayer acts as a barrier to the diffusion of ions and charged molecules. These particles pass into or out of cells through protein molecules which span the lipid bilayer in much the same manner as bridges, tunnels, or ferries permit access to an island. In the case of the cell or cell organelle, these proteins serve to facilitate the transport of charged or polar molecules from the aqueous fluid phase bathing one side of the plasma membrane, through the hydrophobic, nonpolar domain of the inner core of the lipid bilayer, to the aqueous solution on the other side of the membrane.

The proteins which facilitate this transport are classified as "ion

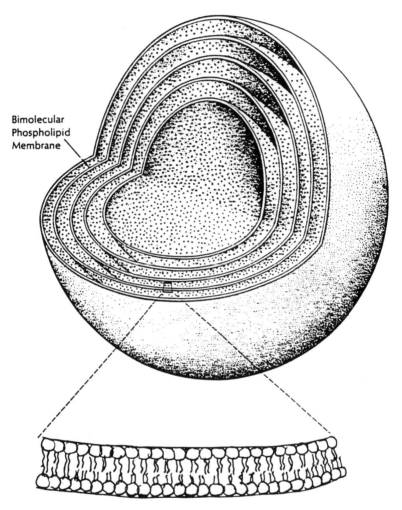

Bimolecular
Phospholipid
Membrane

Fig. 2. The panel on the left is a schematic diagram of a liposome with multiple lamellae each composed of a lipid bilayer. (Modified from G. Weissmann and R. Claiborne, eds., *Cell Membranes, Biochemistry, Cell Biology and Pathology.* HP Publishing Co., Inc., (New York 1975.) The panel on the right is a freeze fracture electron micrograph of an egg phosphatidylcholine liposome. (Kindly provided by A. Janoff, The Liposome Company Inc., Princeton, NJ; magnification 180,000 X).

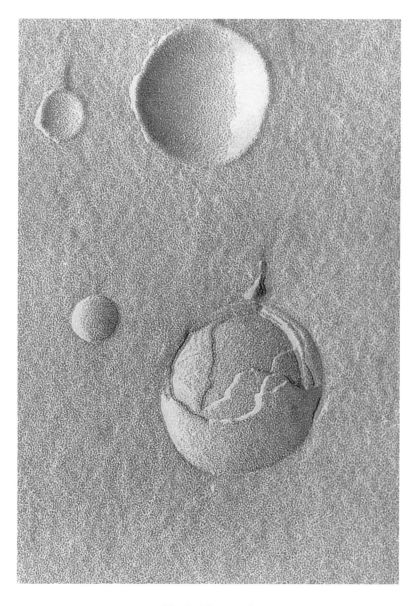

Fig. 2. (*Continued*)

channels," "pumps," and "transport proteins." These transport proteins differ considerably in their structure and function. First let's consider *ion channels*. An ion channel is a single large protein molecule or oligomer which spans the plasma membrane. Some ion channel proteins can be visualized by very high magnification microscopy. We can study their behavior by a technique called "patch clamping." Patch clamping permits the study of the behavior of single proteins (or oligomers) by recording the minute quantities of current carried by ions which pass through the transmembrane channels.

This is how it works. A micropipette filled with an electrolyte solution, with a tip diameter of about 1 to 2 micrometers (.00004 of an inch) is placed against the plasma membrane of a cell. Gentle suction is applied; a small "patch" of membrane is sucked up against the tip of the pipette and forms a tight "bond" with the pipette tip. The "patch" may be left as part of the cell membrane or pulled out of the cell membrane. Since the patch of membrane is very small and ion channels are sparsely distributed in the plasma membrane, a "patch" usually contains only a single ion channel. The pipette, filled with an electrolyte solution, serves as a resistance electrode which permits the measurement of the minute amount of electric current that results when ions move through the ion channel. The channels are not fixed in their shape or electric charge. Channels "open and close" in response to a variety of stimuli. When a channel is "open" a fixed quantity of current flows. It is estimated that 10^7 to 10^8 ions/s pass through an "open" ion channel. The channel opens and closes in an "all-or-none" fashion and the length of time it is "open" is variable. If the patch contains two channels, twice the current is seen when both channels are open. Figure 3 is an example of a patch clamp recording.

Ion channels which open and close in response to chemical stimuli (agonists) are termed "receptor-operated" channels. The stimulus acts on a protein, a receptor, closely associated with the ion channel, to either open or close the channel. Other channels open or close in response to changes in the voltage across the plasma membrane ("voltage dependent channels").

Many different ion channels have been identified by patch clamp and other techniques. Some of these ion channels are highly specific for a

Fig. 3. Patch clamp electrical recording. This tracing records the activity of a single K^+ channel from brain tissue. Time lines are 100 ms. Note that while the frequency and duration of channel opening is variable, the current (the height of deflection) is constant, suggesting passage of ions through a single channel. (Courtesy of Drs. Bruce Cherksey and Victor Sapirstein.)

given ion such as sodium or calcium. Others are only relatively specific permitting positive- or negative-charged ions only.

It is important to recognize that an ion channel permits the net movement of an ion only *in the direction of its electrochemical gradient*. When considering the movement of *charged* particles (ions) it is not only the difference in actual concentration of the ion across the cell membrane that is important. There is an electrical potential difference between the inner (cytoplasmic) and outer aspects of most cell membranes. The lipid bilayer acts as an "electrical insulator" permitting a voltage to be maintained across the cell membrane; in electrical terms, the membrane has low capacitance. In most mammalian cells the cytoplasm is electronegative; the membrane potential is usually -50 to -60 mV. This potential difference is the result of the unequal distribution of one or more ions across the membrane. This unequal distribution may be the result of the passive diffusion of ions across the cell membrane or the active transport of charged molecules or ions (electrogenic transport).

The Nernst equation (which is based solely on physicochemical principles) predicts that at $25°C$, with a membrane potential difference of -59 mV, the passive distribution of any monovalent cation across the cell membrane should lead to a tenfold greater concentration within the cell. The ratio of extracellular to intracellular concentration of potassium approximates this prediction. This is attributed to the great permeability of the plasma membrane to potassium. Potassium crosses the plasma membrane through potassium channels.

The intracellular concentrations of ions such as sodium, hydrogen, and calcium are far below that predicted by the Nernst equation. Each of these ions is actively transported out of the cell, and an electrochemical gradient favoring influx is thereby created. The gradient is maintained by the relative impermeability of the lipid bilayer plasma membrane.

When specific channels in the plasma membrane are "opened" by receptor-agonist interaction or a transmembrane voltage change, the electrochemical gradient is the driving force for ion movement into or out of the cell. Movement through channels is always in the direction of the electrochemical gradient.

"Pumps" are transport proteins which can move polar molecules or charged particles across membranes against their electrochemical gradient, that is, "uphill." These proteins, often larger than ion channels, also span the plasma membrane. The hallmark of membrane pumps is a requirement for energy expenditure.

Primary active transport pumps derive the energy to drive transport from the enzymatic cleavage of adenosine triphosphate (ATP). Two primary pumps will be described in some detail.

The H^+ ATPase, the proton pump (described on pages 34–35), utilizes the energy derived from the enzymatic splitting of ATP to transport hydrogen ions against an electrochemical gradient.

Na^+K^+ ATPase, the sodium pump (pages 24–25), uses the energy derived from splitting ATP to transport two potassium ions into the cell and three sodium ions out of the cell for each molecule of ATP hydrolyzed. This membrane pump is inhibited by the binding of the cardiac glycoside, ouabain, to the external aspect of the membrane protein.

Secondary active transporters are transmembrane proteins which mediate uphill transport utilizing the chemical or electrochemical gradients created by a primary active transporter, usually sodium–potassium ATPase. These transport proteins may facilitate the movement of one or more ions in the same direction (cotransporter or symporter) or may mediate the translocation of two or more ions in opposite directions (antiporter). In either case, the energy derived from the movement of one species *down* its electrochemical gradient appears to energize the uphill transport of one or more other particles. The precise manner in which this energy is "coupled" is not known but may involve phosphorylation and dephosphorylation of carrier proteins which span the plasma membrane. The Na^+-H^+ antiporter, which will be described in more detail (pages 36–37) is an example of an antiporter. The driving force for this transporter is the sodium concentration gradient. The influx of sodium across the cell membrane (down its concentration gradient) provides the energy for H^+ efflux (uphill movement).

The transport protein which exchanges chloride and bicarbonate across the red blood cell membrane is another antiporter. This protein, band 3 protein, has been isolated and extensively characterized. It accounts for 25 percent of the protein of the red blood cell plasma membrane. The driving force for this antiporter is the concentration gradient for bicarbonate. This transporter is inhibited by stilbene disulfonates (SITS or DIDS), which also inhibit other anion transport systems.

An example of cotransport is found in cells which transport Na^+, K^+, and two Cl^- together, utilizing the chemical gradient for sodium as a source of energy. This "triple cotransporter" is responsible for chloride reabsorption in the thick ascending limb of Henle and for chloride secretion in the rectal gland of the dogfish shark. The Na/K/2Cl cotransporter is inhibited by the diuretics which act at the ascending limb of the loop of Henle (furosemide and bumetanide).

The sodium-glucose cotransporter in the proximal renal tubule is an example of a well-defined membrane protein which transports glucose molecules utilizing energy derived from the transmembrane sodium gradient. In the proximal tubular cell of the kidney this transport protein serves to reabsorb filtered glucose from the tubular fluid. In the normal human kidney approximately 250 mg (1.4 mmol) of glucose can be transported each minute, and, since the filtered load of glucose is usually less than 100 mg (0.55 mmol) glucose is reabsorbed completely from the tubular fluid. The sodium-glucose cotransporter is inhibited, competitively, by the drug phlorizin.

5

Sodium, Potassium, Chloride, and the "Trigger Twins," Calcium and Hydrogen

The array of ion channels, pumps, and secondary active transport proteins (antiporters and symporters) in the lipid bilayer plasma membrane serve not only to maintain internal ion concentrations within a narrow range but are also critical for many other cellular functions. The concentration of hydrogen ion within cells plays a critical role in many cytosolic processes and therefore intracellular pH must be closely regulated. What purpose is served by the movement of other ions, such as sodium, potassium, and chloride, into and out of cells? Let's look at the possible functions served by the transport of some of the more common extra- and intracellular electrolytes.

The transport of sodium out of cells, by the Na–K ATPase pump, is one of the major means by which chemical energy is utilized to perform work at a cellular level. The unique role of sodium in this process derives from the impermeability of the lipid bilayer to the sodium ion and the abundance of the enzyme sodium–potassium ATPase which directly couples energy derived from ATP hydrolysis to the uphill transport of sodium ions out of cells. The cytoplasmic concentration of sodium is maintained far below that of the extracellular fluid. Since the efflux of three sodium ions is coupled to the influx of two potassium ions, the process is electrogenic, that is, the cytoplasm is rendered electronegative relative to the bathing medium. By the simple arrangement of an ion pump in an impermeable membrane, active sodium transport provides the driving force for a very wide range of secondary transport processes.

The concentration gradient for sodium (roughly tenfold greater in the extracellular bathing fluid than in the cytoplasm) and the membrane potential difference (generally -60 mV, cytoplasm electronegative) provide a strong electrochemical driving force for sodium entry into cells. This driving force provides the energy for the uphill transport of a variety of substrates and ions through antiporters, symporters, or cotransporters. Substrates such as glucose and amino acids are transported into cells, against a concentration gradient by specific transport proteins (cotransporters) which couple the electrochemical gradient for sodium entry to substrate uptake. Ions such as hydrogen and calcium are transported out of the cell, against their electrochemical potential, by sodium–hydrogen or sodium–calcium exchangers which derive their energy from the sodium gradient. The "triple cotransporter" described earlier, which mediates electroneutral transport of one Na^+, one K^+, and two Cl^- ions across cell membranes, is dependent on the sodium gradient. The gradient is dissipated by transport processes in which sodium enters the cell via a cotransporter or antiporter. The sodium pump utilizes the energy stored as ATP to regenerate the electrochemical gradient which drives these transport processes.

Active sodium transport and secondary sodium cotransport or antiport play an important role in establishing osmotic gradients which determine water movement and thereby are critical for cell volume regulation.

It has been estimated that the sodium pump accounts for 15 to 40 percent of cellular ATP hydrolysis, evidence that the generation and maintenance of the sodium gradient represents a major pathway by which potential energy, stored in the form of ATP, is used to perform work, in the form of transport of substrates or ions against electrochemical gradients. Given the role of sodium transport as "the hydroelectric plant" of the cell, it should be clear that while the intracellular and extracellular concentrations of sodium do not vary greatly, sodium traffic across cell membranes must be considerable to provide for other transport processes.

In bacteria and other prokaryotes, the transmembrane hydrogen ion gradient provides the electrochemical driving force for secondary active transport. This very ancient transport system is still evident in the mitochondrial membranes of vertebrates cells.

Potassium transport is closely linked to membrane transport of sodium. The Na^+-K^+ ATPase directly couples sodium efflux with potassium entry into cells. Sodium ions "recycle" back into the cytoplasm via coupled transport processes. Potassium "recycles" out of the cytoplasm through potassium channels. The frequency of potassium channel opening, and therefore potassium conductance, appears to be closely linked to ATP hydrolysis by Na^+-K^+ ATPase. This provides a co-ordinated system in which sodium ions are cycled across the cell membrane to maintain membrane transport and potassium serves to "rectify" the membrane potential resulting from electrogenic transport. Clearly the transport of sodium and potassium across cell membranes must be fairly closely linked and both ions should be present in abundance to serve these "purposes."

Chloride anion (Cl^-) is also present in abundance; extracellular fluid chloride concentration averages 90 to 110 mmol/L. Aside from the role which chloride serves in maintaining extracellular fluid osmolality and electrical neutrality, chloride plays a critical role in hydrogen ion transport.

In the red blood cell, chloride-bicarbonate exchange facilitates the uptake of CO_2 produced in metabolizing tissues and the release of CO_2 in pulmonary capillaries. This will be described in more detail (see pages 47–49). Considering the large quantity of bicarbonate generated and transported in these systems (roughly 15 mol of CO_2 are excreted by the lungs daily), an abundant exchange ion such as chloride seems a "physiological necessity."

In contrast to Na^+, K^+, and Cl^-, which serve the functions of maintaining membrane potentials, driving membrane transport processes and facilitating cell volume regulation, and which are present in *millimolar* $(10^{-3} M)$ concentrations, the intracellular concentrations of hydrogen ion and calcium ion are in the range $10^{-7} M$ to $10^{-8} M$. For both H^+ and Ca^{2+} an electrochemical gradient favors entry into cells.

While the very low concentrations of hydrogen and calcium make them unsuitable ions to generate membrane potentials or drive membrane transport processes, the ability of these ions to interact with cellular proteins endows them with unique properties. We have already considered the remarkable array of biologic effects that are mediated by changes in intracellular hydrogen ion concentration—changes in enzyme activity, ion channel conductance, hemoglobin affinity for oxygen, cell growth, and DNA replication. These effects are mediated by relatively small changes in intracellular hydrogen ion concentration. Changes in intracellular ionized calcium concentration also mediate a wide variety of cellular processes. Hydrogen ion and calcium ion appear to exhibit a striking parallelism as intracellular ions (Table 5.1).

Table 5.1. Hydrogen Ion and Calcium Ion "The Trigger Twins"

H^+	Ca^{2+}
H^+ ion is buffered by binding to intracellular buffers (weak acids and bases)	Ca^{2+} is "buffered" by binding to intracellular calcium-binding proteins
H^+ ions are actively transported across microsomal membranes and across the plasma membranes of some cells by a specific H^+ ATPase (proton pump)	Ca^{2+} ions are actively transported across microsomal membranes and the plasma membrane by a specific Ca^{2+} ATPase (calcium pump)
H^+ exchanges across the cell membrane for sodium (Na^+–H^+ exchanger)	Ca^{2+} exchanges across the cell membrane for sodium (Na^+–Ca^{2+} exchanger)
Agonists result in rapid changes in intracellular $[H^+]$ by changing Na^+–H^+ antiporter activity	Agonists result in rapid changes in intracellular $[Ca^{2+}]$ by opening calcium channels or releasing Ca^{2+} from bound stores
Changes in intracellular $[H^+]$ alter the shape of proteins and thereby change enzyme activity, protein–protein interactions, and channel conductance	Changes in intracellular $[Ca^{2+}]$ induce shape changes in many proteins resulting in the activation or inactivation of enzymes and changes in the state of contractile proteins

This comparison suggests that the very low and exquisitely regulated intracellular concentrations of H^+ and Ca^{2+} reflect the role that these ions play in activating or regulating the activity of intracellular proteins, that is, both H^+ and Ca^{2+} function as intracellular signals. The "fine tuning" which is required in the regulation of intracellular events is probably accounted for by the efficiency of intracellular buffering of hydrogen ion and intracellular sequestration (a close equivalent of buffering) of calcium ion, and the presence of transport proteins which drive hydrogen and calcium ions out of cells.

6

Getting the H$^+$ Out of the Cell: The Proton Pump and the Na$^+$–H$^+$ Exchanger

We are now ready to examine the mechanisms which serve to control intracellular hydrogen ion concentration.

Intracellular hydrogen ion concentration has been measured or estimated in a variety of ways—by the distribution of weak acids and bases across cell membranes, with pH-sensitive intracellular electrodes, by nuclear magnetic resonance (NMR) spectroscopy, and most recently, by use of intracellular pH-sensitive fluorescent molecules. With increasing refinement of techniques for measurement of intracellular pH, it has become apparent that considerable heterogeneity of pH exists among intracellular organelles. The contents of lysosomal vesicles are acidified to a pH of 4 to 5 by H$^+$ ATPase. The acid environment in these specialized vesicles serves specific cellular functions such as the activation of acid hydrolases and the dissociation of receptor-agonist complexes. In most cells "average" cytosolic hydrogen ion concentration is maintained within a very narrow range, pH ranging from 6.9 to 7.3. This requires "active" transport of hydrogen ions out of the cell since

1. The potential difference across the membrane favors the passive movement of hydrogen ion into the cell. Passive distribution of H$^+$ across the cell membrane with a potential difference of -59 mV (negative inside) would result in an intracellular hydrogen ion concentration tenfold greater than in the bathing fluid; this would result in an intracellular

29

hydrogen ion concentration of 400 nM or pH 6.4. Intracellular pH is lower than extracellular pH in all animals and, in general, is quite close to the neutral pH of water.

2. Hydrogen ion is *generated* within the cell by metabolic processes.

3. For unicellular organisms and freshwater multicellular organisms, including invertebrates and vertebrates such as fish and amphibia, the hydrogen ion concentration of the external environment may be relatively high and favor passive diffusion of H^+ into cells.

The ability to regulate intracellular $[H^+]$ is so crucial that it is not surprising that we can find mechanisms for pH regulation in very primitive single-cell organisms such as algae and bacteria.

How is the concentration of hydrogen ion within the cell regulated?

The most immediate mechanism which serves to stabilize intracellular H^+ concentration is buffering.

Buffering is a property of weak acids and weak bases, that is, acids and bases which are not completely ionized in aqueous solution. When protons (or hydroxyl ions) are added to a solution containing a buffer, chemical reactions occur which neutralize some of the added protons (or hydroxyl ions). As a result, the pH changes less than if the buffer were not present. An example of a buffer acid:

$$Buffer - H \leftrightarrow buffer^- + H^+$$

When H^+ is added, some of the added H^+ combines with buffer$^-$

$$Buffer^- + H^+ \rightarrow buffer - H$$

For a weak acid buffer system, such as acetic acid/acetate, the equilibrium can be described by the equation

$$HAc \times K = [Ac^-] \times [H^+] \quad \text{or} \quad K = \frac{[Ac^-] \times [H^+]}{[HAc]}$$

Taking the log of both sides,

$$\log K = \log \frac{[Ac^-][H^+]}{[HAc]}$$

and rearranging,

$$-\log[H^+] = -\log K + \log \frac{[Ac^-]}{[HAc]}$$

but, $-\log[H^+] = pH$ and, by analogy with pH, we write pK instead of $-\log K$:

$$pH = pK + \log \frac{[Ac^-]}{[HAc]}$$

This is the Henderson–Hasselbalch equation.
The pK of a weak acid or base is the pH at which

$$\frac{[Base]}{[Acid]} = 1 \qquad (\log \text{ of } 1 = 0)$$

The buffering of a weak acid or base is maximal at its pK. The reason for this can be seen if we realize that at a pH 1 unit below the pK the ratio of $[Ac^-]/[HAc] = \frac{1}{10} (\log \frac{1}{10} = -1)$ and at a pH 1 unit above the pK, $[Ac^-]/[HAc] = 10 (\log 10 = 1)$. In other words, at a pH 1 unit below the pK 91 percent of the buffer is in the form of the undissociated acid, at a pH 1 unit above the pK 91 percent of the buffer is in the form of dissociated conjugate base. The notable exception to this rule is the HCO_3^-/CO_2 buffer system which buffers extracellular fluid at a pH of 7.4 despite a pK of 6.1. The effectiveness of the bicarbonate system in buffering a pH so far removed from its pK is related to the "open" nature of the bicarbonate system (see pages 68–69).

Within cells, the major buffers are bicarbonate (HCO_3^-/H_2CO_3), proteins, and phosphate ($HPO_4^{2-}/H_2PO_4^-$). When hydrogen ion is buffered within the cell, protons which combine with bicarbonate form H_2CO_3

$$H^+ + HCO_3^- \rightarrow H_2CO_3$$

In the presence of carbonic anhydrase, H_2CO_3 is broken down to CO_2 and water; the CO_2 diffuses out of the cell. H_2CO_3 does not accumulate; a molecule of bicarbonate is lost for each proton buffered. Protons which combine with other buffers, phosphates or proteins, are retained. Proteins act as buffers by virtue of the amino and carboxyl groups of their component amino acids. Since the intracellular concentrations of bicarbonate and phosphate are relatively low, the bulk of intracellular H^+ buffering is attributable to protein. Most carboxyl groups and amino groups have pK values which are far removed from intracellular pH and do not contribute to buffering protons. Histidine, whose imidazole group has a pK 6.4 to 7.0, is the buffer most ideally suited for buffering [H^+] in the range of intracellular pH.

$$
\begin{array}{ccc}
R & & R \\
| & & | \\
CH_2 & & CH_2 \\
| & & | \\
HC{=}C & \leftrightarrow & HC{=}C \quad + H^+ \\
| \quad | & & | \quad | \\
{}^+HN \quad NH & & N \quad NH \\
\diagdown\diagup & & \diagdown\diagup \\
CH & & CH
\end{array}
$$

Faced with an acid load, cellular buffers bind H^+ and minimize the change in [H^+]. The maintenance of constant intracellular pH, however, requires that the buffered H^+ ion be eliminated and that new bicarbonate buffer be generated. This necessitates hydrogen ion secretion.

Hydrogen ion secretion serves to eliminate buffered H^+ and to regenerate bicarbonate. The extracellular [H^+] of unicellular organisms is highly variable and generally favors H^+ entry into the cell. In multicellular organisms, under most circumstances, the electrochemical gradient also favors passive diffusion of H^+ from the extracellular bathing fluid into cells. H^+ ion secretion, therefore, is "uphill" requiring transport processes which can operate against concentration gradients or electrochemical gradients for H^+ ion.

Two different H^+ ion transport systems play a role in the regulation of intracellular pH. The first is an H^+-ATPase or (proton-translocating ATPase); the second is an exchanger or antiporter which transports a H^+ ion in one direction and another cation—usually sodium—in the opposite direction. The H^+-ATPase utilizes the energy derived from the enzymatic hydrolysis of ATP to actively transport hydrogen ion; the antiporter utilizes the sodium gradient generated by another active pump (Na^+–K^+ ATPase).

Let's look at the H^+-ATPase pump first. H^+-ATPase consists of a group of proteins located within the lipid bilayer plasma membrane. It consists of several subunits. Within the membrane, subunits whose molecular weight is about 15 kDa form an "ion channel." This is connected via other proteins called the "stalk" to a cluster of globular protein subunits, on the inner (cytoplasmic) aspect of the cell membrane, collectively termed the "catalytic unit." These membrane pumps can be visualized in negatively stained electron photomicrographs.

H^+-ATPase with subunits arranged in this general manner have been identified in cell membranes of bacteria, yeast, and renal tubular cells and in the membranes that surround intracellular organelles such as mitochondria, chloroplasts, lysosomes, endosomes, and secretory vesicles. While the proteins differ somewhat depending on the source, there is a remarkable similarity in the composition of the catalytic units among very primitive bacteria and mammalian cells indicating that these proteins evolved very early and have been preserved—and have subserved similar functions—for millennia.

The enzymatic cleavage of ATP by the catalytic unit of H^+-ATPase provides the energy to transport hydrogen ions out of the cell through the membrane "channel" against an electrochemical gradient. Since only a proton is transported, that is, there is no cotransport or countertransport ion, the process is electrogenic. The transport of a positively charged H^+ out of the cell increases the electronegativity of the cytoplasm. The H^+-ATPase pump can be inhibited by drugs such as N-ethylmaleimide (NEM) and bafilomycin A.

Incidentally, this same pump can be made to work in the reverse direction to synthesize ATP. If the electrochemical gradient favoring entry of H^+ into the cell is so great that it exceeds the energy released by ATP hydrolysis, H^+ will move in the reverse direction—through the membrane "channel" in the direction of the catalytic unit—and will result in ADP phosphorylation to ATP. The translocation of protons across the lipid bilayer membranes of organelles, such as mitochondria and chloroplasts, is responsible for ATP synthesis; in this mode, the H^+-ATPase transport protein is termed ATP synthase. Nothing succeeds like excess!

H^+-ATPase pumps have been studied extensively in the epithelium of the turtle bladder and the collecting tubule of the mammalian kidney. In these tissues, H^+-ATPase pumps are located on the apical membrane of cells rich in carbonic anhydrase. These remarkable pumps can be regulated—to increase or decrease the rate of H^+ ion pumping—in several ways.

Small vesicles, whose membranes also contain H^+-ATPase pumps, are present in the cytosol below the apical membrane of these cells. Under some circumstances it appears that additional pumps can be inserted into the cell membrane by the fusion of intracellular vesicles with the plasma membrane. Increased CO_2 in the medium bathing these cells induces the fusion of these vesicles with the plasma membrane (exocytosis), and in this way, additional hydrogen-secreting pumps are inserted into the membrane. The mechanism of CO_2-mediated exocytosis appears to involve several steps. CO_2 diffuses freely into the epithelial cell and, catalyzed by carbonic anhydrase, results in intracellular acidification. Increased intracellular $[H^+]$ causes closing of pH-sensitive potassium channels; the result is membrane depolarization and Ca^{2+} influx through voltage-dependent calcium channels. Exocytosis of vesicles and fusion with the plasma membrane is mediated by increased intracellular calcium.

The transport of hydrogen ion by H^+-ATPase is electrogenic, generating both a hydrogen ion gradient and a membrane potential. When hydrogen ion is actively transported out of a cell, intracellular $[H^+]$ decreases and the cell becomes more electronegative. The electrochemical gradient ultimately limits the further pumping of H^+.

Factors which dissipate either the hydrogen ion or electrical gradient generated by H^+-ATPase facilitate H^+ transport. In vesicles which contain H^+-ATPase, chloride entry through chloride channels allows dissipation of the membrane potential; this facilitates hydrogen ion secretion and marked acidification of these cytoplasmic vesicles. In this way chloride transport (via a channel) "functions" to permit active H^+ secretion.

Conversely, if the proton-secreting cell is bathed in a medium which buffers the secreted protons and prevents the buildup of a hydrogen ion gradient, hydrogen ion secretion will be facilitated. This "facilitation by buffering" assumes an important role in the kidney tubule where the luminal fluid bathing renal tubular cells may be rich in bicarbonate.

The second type of H^+ transport protein is termed a sodium–hydrogen antiporter. These proteins are found in the plasma membranes of most animal cells, both epithelial cells specialized for ion transport and non-transporting cells such as vascular smooth muscle cells and fibroblasts. The sodium–hydrogen antiporters are a family of related proteins with multiple hydrophobic membrane-spanning segments and hydrophilic extracellular and intracellular ion-binding sites. A cytoplasmic carboxy-terminal sequence appears to be the site of regulation of the activity of the exchanger. The sodium–hydrogen antiporter serves to permit the outward transport of H^+ ion utilizing the energy derived from the inward movement of sodium down the chemical gradient created by the active extrusion of Na^+ by Na^+–K^+ ATPase. The stoichiometry of the Na^+–H^+ exchanger is 1:1, therefore it is an *electroneutral* process. No transport of hydrogen occurs if sodium is removed from the bathing medium or if Na^+–K^+ ATPase is inhibited by ouabain. The sodium–hydrogen antiporter is inhibited by the potassium-sparing diuretic, amiloride.

The activity of the sodium–hydrogen antiporter is subject to regulation both by changes in intracellular hydrogen ion concentration and in response to a variety of extracellular stimuli or agonists. A regulatory site on the cytoplasmic portion of the antiporter is highly sensitive to the $[H^+]$ of the cytoplasm. An increase in cytosolic H^+ concentration accelerates antiporter activity; a decrease inhibits antiporter activity. The kinetics of the response of Na^+–H^+ exchanger to increased intracellular hydrogen ion concentration suggest that increased hydrogen ion transport is not due simply to the greater quantity of hydrogen ion available for transport at the cytoplasmic binding site but rather that the transport protein is itself, in some way, activated. It is reasonable to speculate that a change in intracellular hydrogen ion concentration induces a conformational change at the cytoplasmic site of the exchange protein which accelerates the exchange process. The extracellular portion of the exchanger is relatively insensitive to differences in H$^+$ concentration.

This remarkable regulatory site also functions to diminish Na$^+$–H$^+$ exchange when cytoplasmic hydrogen ion concentration falls below a critical level. The net effect is a hydrogen transport system which "accelerates" sharply when there is a stimulus for hydrogen ion extrusion and is limited by a "governor" which turns the system off before hydrogen ion concentration falls below a critical level. Both the stimulus—hydrogen ion—and the effector—the Na$^+$–H$^+$ antiporter—are contained within a single cell. This regulation of Na$^+$–H$^+$ exchange can be viewed as a means of maintaining intracellular hydrogen ion concentration within narrow limits. The signal for increased activity of the exchanger is an increase in cellular hydrogen ion concentration. The response is increased proton efflux to maintain cell pH.

The activity of the Na$^+$–H$^+$ antiporter is also modulated by external stimuli. A number of polypeptide substances including circulating hormones, such as parathyroid hormone and antidiuretic hormone, angiotensin II, and growth factors, such as epithelial growth factor (EGF) and platelet derived growth factor (PDGF), act on cell surface receptors to effect Na$^+$–H$^+$ antiporter activity. These agonists act via "second messengers," substances released into the cytosol or activated in the plasma membrane as a consequence of receptor occupancy. Some agonists activate membrane-bound adenylate cyclase and result in the production of cyclic AMP and possibly the activation of membrane calcium channels. Other agonists activate membrane phospholipase C which catalyzes the enzymatic cleavage of membrane phosphoinositol to diacylglycerol and inositol triphosphate; these facilitate the release of calcium from the endoplasmic reticulum, a storehouse of bound calcium. The two "second messengers," cyclic AMP and ionized calcium, activate enzymes (protein kinases) which transfer the terminal phosphate of ATP to target proteins. Phosphorylation of specific amino acids (tyrosine, threonine, or serine) on target proteins such as the Na^+-H^+ exchanger modulates the configuration and activity of the target protein. Three different protein kinases are known to regulate the activity of the Na^+-H^+ antiporter, namely, protein kinase C (activated by diacylglycerol), cyclic AMP-dependent protein kinase (activated by cyclic AMP), and calmodulin kinase II (activated by ionized calcium). Changes in Na^+-H^+ antiporter activity induced by agonists do not play a major role in acid–base balance. Receptor-stimulated Na^+-H^+ antiporter activity can be viewed as a means of signaling, via changes in the cellular concentration of the "trigger twins" H^+ and Ca^{2+}.

While H^+ and Ca^{2+} appear to play important roles as "triggers," the intracellular events so triggered are almost universally mediated by the action of kinases which transfer phosphate groups from ATP to enzymes, resulting in either increased or decreased enzyme activity. This process is termed *signal transduction*. Why does phosphate play such a key role in this process? While this question cannot be answered definitively, and is, in fact, the subject of very active investigation at this time, I would like to offer a speculation.

The activation or inactivation of enzymes and the opening and closing of channels are likely related to changes in the shape or configuration of enzymes or membrane proteins. Theoretically, such changes in protein configuration could result from many different reactions. Significant changes in the configuration of proteins results from the formation or breaking of peptide bonds but these reactions are virtually irreversible. The generation of fibrin from fibrinogen, or the octapeptide angiotensin II from the decapeptide angiotensin I, represents an example of the "one-way" breaking of peptide bonds in changing protein structure or activity.

Modulated reactions, those that must be reversibly turned on and off easily, are more likely brought about by the addition or removal of side groups which, by virtue of their size or charge, effect the tertiary or quaternary configuration of proteins. As pointed out earlier, addition or removal of a proton from amino acid side chains may induce shape changes in polypeptides or proteins. However, the number of reactive groups which are capable of binding protons, within the physiologic pH range, is somewhat limited. Furthermore, the hydrogen ion is small and carries only a single charge. By contrast, the phosphate group $PO_4{}^{3-}$ is both large and highly charged and would be expected to alter the tertiary structure of proteins more markedly than the addition or loss of a proton.

Protein kinases, many linked to cell membrane receptors, serve to transfer phosphate groups from ATP to a number of amino acids. Specific kinases transfer phosphate to tyrosine, serine, and threonine. These amino acids are widely abundant in polypeptides and proteins. Both the source of the phosphate and the energy for its transfer reside in the high-energy phosphate of ATP. Another class of enzymes, phosphatases, cleave phosphate groups from specific amino acids. In this way, the multiple kinases together with ATP constitute a rapidly responsive system by which a variety of signals can be translated into changes in intracellular protein shape with resultant changes in enzyme activity or membrane configuration.

> Having considered the transport processes which account for the secretion of hydrogen ions, we must now answer the question,
>
> What is the source of the hydrogen ions which are secreted by cells?

As described earlier (pp. 29–30) protons are generated by cellular metabolic processes. The membrane potential difference favors the inward diffusion of hydrogen ions. CO_2 diffuses freely across the cell membrane and is hydrated to H_2CO_3 which dissociates to yield H^+ and $HCO_3{}^-$. Cellular buffering, however, serves to maintain a relatively fixed concentration of hydrogen ions in the cytosol. Most of the hydrogen ion secreted via the proton pump or the Na^+–H^+ exchanger must be generated within the cell. The zinc-containing enzyme, carbonic anhydrase, plays a central role in this process. Carbonic anhydrase catalyzes two closely related reactions:

$$CO_2 + H_2O \leftrightarrow H_2CO_3 \qquad \text{(the hydration of } CO_2\text{)}$$

and

$$CO_2 + OH^- \leftrightarrow HCO_3{}^- \qquad \text{(the hydroxylation of } CO_2\text{)}$$

The hydroxylation of CO_2 is pH dependent since the concentration of OH^- ion is inversely related to the concentration of H^+ ion. This reaction is thought to predominate where intracellular pH is high, that is, in cells which are specialized for acid secretion. Though both reactions can proceed without a catalyst, carbonic anhydrase greatly accelerates both reactions. Carbonic anhydrase has the highest molar activity of any known enzyme. It is estimated that under optimal conditions 36,000,000 molecules of CO_2 are hydrated per minute by a single molecule of carbonic anhydrase! Just as hydrogen ATPases appear very early in the evolutionary scheme, carbonic anhydrase analogs, similar to those of man and other mammals, are present in primitive vertebrates.

The generation of H_2CO_3 within the cell, from CO_2 generated by metabolic activity or CO_2 which diffuses into the cell, provides a source of H^+ for secretion via the reaction

$$H_2CO_3 \rightarrow H^+ + HCO_3^-$$

The dissociation of H_2CO_3 also yields a bicarbonate ion which must exit the cell. Similarly the hydroxylation of CO_2, while removing hydroxyl ions and thereby facilitating the dissociation of H_2O to yield H^+, also generates bicarbonate ion. Consideration of the transport of bicarbonate requires us to shift our focus from single cells to more polarized groups of cells such as epithelial tissues.

Cells that are organized as tissues display polarity of the plasma membrane. In epithelial tissues, the surface which faces the lumen of tubules (as in the kidney or intestine) or the external environment (as in gills or sweat glands) is termed the apical surface. The apical surface often consists of many small villous projections, the *brush border*, which serves to greatly increase the surface area. The remainder of the plasma membrane, including those portions that rest on the supporting basal lamina and those portions on the sides of the cell abutting adjacent cells, is termed the *basolateral surface*.

There is striking heterogeneity in the distribution of membrane proteins between the apical and basolateral regions. The heterogeneity in transport proteins and channels accounts for the ability of epithelial tissues to effect vectorial transport—transport in a single direction—

either secretion or absorption. In epithelial cells, the receptors for hormones or agonists are usually located on the basolateral aspect of the cell where they are exposed to bloodborne substances. The transmembrane signal is transmitted to the transport protein located on the apical or luminal side of the cell.

> Now we can ask, "What becomes of the HCO_3^- when H^+ is secreted?"

H^+ derived from the dissociation of water or H_2CO_3 provides a source of H^+ for transport and leaves a hydroxyl ion (OH^-) or bicarbonate ion (HCO_3^-) in the cytosol. Whether the proton is derived from H_2O or H_2CO_3 makes little difference since carbonic anhydrase also catalyzes the reaction,

$$OH^- + CO_2 \rightarrow HCO_3^-$$

In epithelia specialized for acid secretion, the transport of H^+ ions across the apical or luminal membrane of the cell is precisely mirrored by the efflux of HCO_3^- across the basolateral membrane.

In the proximal tubule of the kidney, the major mechanism responsible for basolateral membrane bicarbonate efflux is a $Na^+/3HCO_3^-$ cotransporter. This is a sodium-dependent, electrogenic transporter. The electrochemical gradient favoring bicarbonate efflux provides the driving force for this transporter. This is a "secondary" transport system since the electrochemical gradient results, in part, from the action of Na^+-K^+ ATPase in generating cytoplasmic electronegativity. This cotransporter is inhibited by disulfonic stilbenes (SITS or DIDS), inhibitors of anion transport. In the collecting tubule basolateral membrane, bicarbonate efflux occurs by a sodium-independent, electroneutral, chloride/HCO_3^- exchange. The transport protein on the basolateral membrane of cells of the collecting tubule has not been fully characterized but appears to have considerable homology with a well-characterized anion exchange protein, the band 3 protein, of the erythrocyte membrane. Band 3 protein, so named because of its electrophoretic mobility, is a 95-kDa protein which constitutes almost 25 percent of the red blood cell membrane protein. It is estimated that there are about 1 million copies of this molecule on each erythrocyte. This exchange protein exhibits a high degree of anion specificity; the affinity for chloride is one million fold greater than that for the cation potassium.

The direction of the 1:1 chloride-bicarbonate exchange is determined by small changes in the concentration gradient for bicarbonate across the cell membrane. This can be predicted from a consideration of the membrane potential gradient and the relative cytoplasmic and extracellular concentrations of chloride and bicarbonate. Intracellular chloride and bicarbonate concentrations are both well below that in plasma, that is, chemical gradients favor the influx of both anions. The potential difference across the cell membrane, negative on the internal aspect, favors anion efflux. The distribution of chloride across most cell membranes is quite close to that predicted by passive distribution or, stated differently, the concentration gradient favoring chloride influx almost exactly balances the potential gradient favoring efflux. As a consequence of the offsetting chemical and electrical gradients for chloride, small changes in the chemical gradient for bicarbonate determine whether bicarbonate exits or enters the cell. When intracellular bicarbonate concentration increases, the chemical gradient for bicarbonate favors electroneutral 1:1 bicarbonate efflux and chloride entry. When intracellular bicarbonate concentration is reduced, the same anion exchanger serves to facilitate bicarbonate entry and chloride efflux. The anion exchanger in kidney tubule cells, like that in the erythrocyte, is inhibited by the anion exchange inhibitors, disulfonic stilbenes (SITS, DIDS).

What is the fate of the chloride ion which enters the erythrocyte- or acid-transporting epithelium?

In the red blood cell, protons (generated when CO_2 enters the erythrocyte) and chloride exit, down an electrochemical gradient, through the band 3 anion exchanger. In renal proximal tubular cells, chloride exits via a sodium-dependent $Cl^- - HCO_3^-$ exchanger (1 Na^+, 2 HCO_3^- in/1 Cl^- out) or a $K^+ - Cl^-$ cotransporter. In other renal tubular segments (e.g., the thick ascending limb of Henle) chloride exits via basolateral chloride channels.

7

The Milieu Interieur

So far we have been considering the transport of hydrogen ion and electrolytes across the membranes of single cells as such transport might occur in unicellular organisms—cells separated by a plasma membrane from a bathing medium whose composition is relatively constant and not significantly changed by the secreted acid. The main requirements for maintaining constant intracellular hydrogen ion concentration are the ability to buffer hydrogen ion and, ultimately, to excrete hydrogen ion at a rate equal to the rate at which hydrogen ion accumulates in the cell by entry through the plasma membrane or metabolic production. Generally the "bathing medium" of unicellular organisms, that is, lakes, streams, rivers or oceans, is very large in volume relative to the cellular volume. The quantity of hydrogen ion secreted has little effect on the hydrogen ion concentration of the medium.

The situation is somewhat different when we consider multicellular terrestrial organisms such as man. Early in evolution, when multicellular organisms developed and emerged from the bodies of water in which they lived, they carried with them a portion of the medium in which cells are bathed. This is what we call the extracellular or interstitial fluid. In very simple or primitive multicellular organisms this extracellular fluid bathes all the cells by a kind of ebb and flow, in more advanced organisms it is actually propelled by a variety of "pumps." Eventually a system of blood vessels and heart evolved as a specialized portion of the extracellular fluid.

The important feature of the extracellular fluid in terrestrial organisms is its relatively small volume relative to the intracellular fluid volume as compared to the "extracellular" volume/intracellular volume ratio of unicellular organisms, whether they be in oceans, lakes, or tidal pools.

While it is true that the excretion of acid by unicellular organisms, algae, plankton and even larger multicellular organisms, such as mollusks, amphibia or fish, hardly affects the composition of the streams, lakes, or oceans in which they live, on a larger, global scale, acids produced by the burning of fossil fuels and the decay of organic matter have a marked effect on the composition of large bodies of water.

"Acid rain" is produced by the chemical reaction between gaseous oxides of sulfur and nitrogen emitted into the atmosphere and water in clouds resulting in the formation of dilute sulfuric and nitric acids. Acid rain droplets have a pH as low as 2.6 and account for significant acidification of lakes in areas where the soil is relatively poor in alkaline material such as limestone. On a global level, acid produced by the "metabolism" of fossil fuels results in acidification of the external milieu bathing both plants and animals with marked, often lethal, effects on cellular function. Interestingly, the concept of the earth as a single living organism, formulated as the Gaia Hypothesis by the British scientist James Lovelock in 1979, had its origins 60 years earlier in the writings of Lawrence J. Henderson, who is best remembered today for his formulation of the Henderson–Hasselbalch equation.

The famous nineteenth-century French physiologist Claude Bernard recognized the importance of maintaining constancy of the composition of the extracellular fluid. He termed the extracellular fluid the "milieu interieur." In "Lessons on the Phenomenon of Life Common to Animals and Plants," published in 1878, he wrote "All the vital mechanisms, however valued they may be, have only one object, that of preserving the conditions of life in the internal environment."

The great American physiologist Homer Smith concluded from his studies of the comparative physiology of the kidney in fish, amphibia, and vertebrates that it was the evolution of the kidney's ability to maintain a constant extracellular fluid composition that allowed the successful development of diverse species adapted to very wide extremes of environmental conditions. Smith went beyond Claude Bernard in stating "All the vital mechanisms operate to preserve the constancy of the internal environment, only *because this environment is the last ditch of defense between the living cells that compromise the organism and a hostile world* [emphasis mine]."

The study of acid–base physiology in man and other vertebrates has focused largely on the regulation of hydrogen ion concentration in the *extracellular fluid*. This may seem paradoxic, since it should be clear that cell function is critically dependent on the maintenance of *intracellular* hydrogen ion concentration within a narrow range, but is understandable on both practical and theoretic considerations. Practically, the analytic tools for measuring acid–base parameters such as pH, CO_2 tension, and buffering in extracellular fluids such as blood or plasma have been available for many years. Techniques for assessing intracellular pH and its major determinants are new and often limited to the study of isolated cells or tissues under closely defined conditions. The ability of cellular transport systems to maintain intracellular pH in the face of varying acid or base loads has not been well defined. On a theoretic level, as a consequence of the limited volume of the extracellular fluid, changes in extracellular fluid composition which result from cellular metabolic activities impose limitations on cellular transport. This necessitated the development of specialized organs whose function is to maintain the extracellular fluid electrolyte and hydrogen ion concentration within a very narrow range. The lung and the kidney play the major roles in the regulation of acid–base balance of the extracellular fluid.

It should become clear as we go along that the lung and the kidney employ many of the transport processes which we have described in single cells. One might say of the evolution of terrestrial animals from simple aquatic invertebrates, "they came onto dry land dragging their transport proteins along with them."

Before considering the manner in which the lung and kidney maintain acid–base homeostasis in the extracellular fluid, it will be useful to review the metabolic processes which challenge the delicate balance of intracellular and extracellular hydrogen ion concentration.

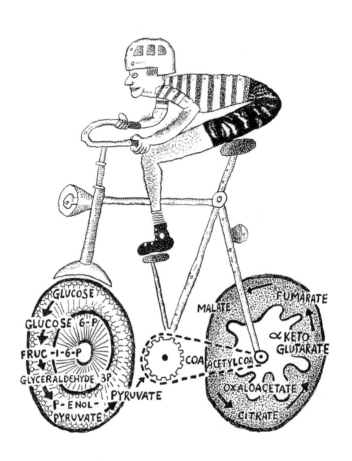

8

Metabolic Acid Production: Metabolic Cycles

The major source of energy for cell metabolism is the oxidation of carbohydrates and fats. Glucose molecules are stored in a very compact form, starch, which is a polymerized form of glucose. When energy is needed, starch can be broken down, catalyzed by the enzyme glycogen phosphorylase, to glucose which enters the metabolic cycle (glycolytic cycle or Embden–Meyerhof pathway) after its energy level is increased by the attachment of a phosphate; this phosphorylation is mediated by the enzyme hexokinase.

The initial phosphorylation and the subsequent introduction of a second phosphate to form fructose 1,6-phosphate supply the activation energy which allows the subsequent steps of the glycolytic pathway to proceed in a "downhill" manner.

Compared to the energy produced, very little energy is required to get the reaction started. ATP is the major energy storage form in cells. Two molecules of ATP are utilized in activating glycolysis. Thirty-six molecules of ATP are generated by the complete oxidation of a molecule of glucose to CO_2 and water.

$$C_6H_{12}O_6 + 6O_2 \rightarrow 6CO_2 + 6H_2O$$

Very little of the energy generated by this process is consumed in disposing of the "waste products" CO_2 and water. To some extent both are "recycled" but the bulk of metabolically generated CO_2 is excreted by the lungs. CO_2 is potentially an acid because it can be hydrated to H_2CO_3 which ionizes to yield H^+. CO_2 diffuses rapidly out of cells into peripheral capillaries and out of pulmonary capillaries into pulmonary alveoli. The concentration gradients required to accomplish this transfer of CO_2 are exceedingly small. However, carbon dioxide has a limited solubility in plasma; at the partial pressure of carbon dioxide in tissues only about 8 percent of the total CO_2 transported could be carried as dissolved CO_2 in plasma. A small fraction of CO_2 is transported chemically bound to hemoglobin as carbaminohemoglobin. The bulk of carbon dioxide is transported in capillary blood as bicarbonate. This is achieved by means of the rapid, coordinated actions of carbonic anhydrase and the erythrocyte band-3 bicarbonate–chloride anion exchanger.

Viewed as a "macrotransport system," blood passing through peripheral capillaries, with a capillary transit time of only 4 to 5 seconds, must release oxygen bound to hemoglobin and take up metabolically generated carbon dioxide. CO_2 in plasma diffuses freely across the erythrocyte membrane and is hydrated, catalyzed by carbonic anhydrase, to form H_2CO_3 which ionizes to yield HCO_3^- and H^+. Intracellular bicarbonate concentration increases and bicarbonate exits in exchange for chloride through the anion exchanger to be transported as bicarbonate in plasma. The hydrogen ion binds to and is buffered by the histidine side chain of hemoglobin, decreasing the affinity of hemoglobin for oxygen and facilitating the release of oxygen (Bohr effect).

At the pulmonary capillary, during a similarly brief capillary transit, the reverse sequence occurs. As CO_2 diffuses out of plasma into the alveolus, H^+ dissociates from histidine and combines with bicarbonate to form H_2CO_3 which is rapidly dehydrated to CO_2 for release into alveoli. Intracellular bicarbonate concentration falls and the balance of driving forces for erythrocyte anion efflux is shifted to favor chloride efflux and bicarbonate entry. In this manner plasma bicarbonate is "transformed" into CO_2 to be removed by ventilation. The release of H^+ from hemoglobin increases the binding affinity for oxygen uptake.

This well-orchestrated "macrotransport system" allows the lung to excrete 15,000 mmol/day of CO_2. CO_2 is transported largely in the form of bicarbonate generated in the red blood cell and transported into the plasma—"the bicarbonate shuttle." It is not surprising that early investigators proposed the name capnophorin (gr, = carrier of smoke) for the band 3 protein.

The major portion of *nonvolatile acid* produced by metabolism is derived from the hepatic catabolism of amino acids. The carboxyl group of amino acids yields a bicarbonate ion, and the amino group, an ammonium ion. The remainder of the carbon "backbone" is utilized to generate glucose (gluconeogenesis) or smaller fragments for further oxidation.

Ureagenesis, which is closely linked to amino acid catabolism, converts the HCO_3^- (a conjugate base) and NH_4^+ (a weak conjugate acid) to urea with the result that neither an acid nor a base is produced.

$$2NH_4^+ + 2HCO_3^- \rightarrow NH_2-\overset{\overset{\textstyle O}{\|}}{C}-NH_2 + CO_2 + 3H_2O$$

The enzymes requisite for each of these sets of reactions, that is, *glutaminase* which initiates the enzymatic breakdown of glutamine and other amino acids and *carbamoyl phosphate synthetase* (and the enzymes of the urea cycle) which mediate ureagenesis, are localized within the same hepatocytes which line liver sinusoids from the periportal venule to a point close to the pericentral venule.

The precise metabolic controls which link gluconeogenesis to urea-genesis in hepatocytes is not known. It has been suggested that this might be a site of systemic regulation of acid–base balance. Clearly the catabolism of amino acids results in the generation of a large quantity of bicarbonate—estimated to be about 1000 mmol/100 g of protein metabolized. As gluconeogenesis appears to be tightly linked (in a manner not yet understood) to ureagenesis which "titrates" this bicarbonate with an equivalent quantity of protons derived from NH_4^+, the other by-product of amino acid catabolism, the process does not normally affect acid–base balance.

An analogy can be drawn with the metabolic pathways of glucose metabolism. The oxidation of glucose in the cytosol, through the glycolytic cycle, yields pyruvate. Under aerobic conditions, pyruvate enters the mitochondrium and is ultimately metabolized to CO_2 and water via the tricarboxylic acid cycle or is reutilized in gluconeogenesis. Under pathologic anaerobic conditions this "linkage" between the glycolytic cycle and the tricarboxylic acid cycle is disrupted with the production of lactic acid and leads to lactic acidosis.

One might ask whether under some circumstances gluconeogenesis, which results in the production of molar quantities of bicarbonate, could lead to a pathologic "acute metabolic alkalosis," if the linkage with ureagenesis were disrupted? While urea synthesis may be impaired in some forms of liver disease, acute metabolic alkalosis is not observed because the ammonia so generated would accumulate to toxic levels before a significant quantity of bicarbonate accumulated. Blood ammonia concentration is normally $50\,nM/L$ as compared with plasma bicarbonate concentration, 24 to $26\,mM/L$.

The metabolism of most amino acids results in the production of equimolar quantities of HCO_3^- and NH_4^+ which are consumed by urea synthesis and therefore does not present the organism with an "acid load" or a "base load."

ACID PRODUCTION	BASE PRODUCTION
Methionine $\atop$ Cysteine $\;\to 72\,H^+$	Anionic dicarboxylic acids → $100\,HCO_3^-$
Cationic diaminoacids → $138\,H^+$	Dietary organic anions → $60\,HCO_3^-$
Total = 210 mmol	Total = 160 mmol

The average Western diet results in the daily net addition of about 50 mmol of acid, that is, protons which require buffering and excretion. The oxidation of sulfur-containing amino acids—methionine and cysteine—leads to the formation of one molecule of sulfate and two protons. An average diet provides about 36 mmol of cysteine and methionine and generates 72 mmol of protons or "nonvolatile acid." Oxidation of cationic amino acids (lysine, arginine, and histidine) also yields protons estimated to be about 138 mmol. The oxidation of dicarboxylic amino acids (glutamate and aspartate) is estimated to consume 100 mmol of proton. The oxidation of dietary organic anions (acetate, lactate, citrate, etc.) consumes about 60 mmol of protons. The net balance of proton generation and proton consumption yields a total of 50 mmol of nonvolatile acid which are added daily to the body's cellular and extracellular fluid buffers.

For the organism as a whole, the protons generated by metabolism must be buffered and ultimately excreted if H^+ balance is to be maintained. The major component of the extracellular buffer system is the bicarbonate–H_2CO_3 system. As we noted earlier,

$$H^+ + HCO_3^- \rightarrow H_2CO_3 \rightarrow CO_2 + H_2O$$

Buffering of hydrogen ion by bicarbonate yields CO_2 which is removed by the lung; the net effect is a loss of buffer and hydrogen ion. Other buffers also combine with H^+, for example, $H^+ + HPO_4^{-2} \rightarrow H_2PO_4^-$.

$$H^+ + hemoglobin \rightarrow hemoglobin - H^+$$

Hydrogen ion buffered by phosphate or proteins is retained until it is "back titrated" by bicarbonate

$$H_2PO_4^- + HCO_3^- \rightarrow HPO_4^{-2} + CO_2 + H_2O$$

Buffering serves to maintain the extracellular $[H^+]$ within a narrow range, but ultimately the maintenance of acid balance requires the excretion of the generated protons or the generation of base (bicarbonate).

9

Renal Acid Secretion and the Trail of Ammonia

Just as cell membrane hydrogen ion transport systems (H^+-ATPase and Na^+–H^+ exchange) serve to excrete protons and regenerate intracellular buffers in the microcosm of the cell, the kidney serves to excrete H^+ and regenerate buffers in the macrocosm of the extracellular fluid utilizing, in part, the same H^+ ion transport systems.

A simple calculation will show that there is not enough free hydrogen ion in the body to account for the 50 mmol of proton which are excreted daily. A 70-kg person has a total body water of approximately 50 liters. Since the concentration of hydrogen ion, at pH 7.4, is 40 nM/L, the total hydrogen ion of body fluids, (intra- and extracellular) is only 2000 nmol, or 2 μmol (2×10^{-6} M). This represents only 0.004 percent of the daily renal acid excretion.

The excreted hydrogen ions are derived from CO_2,

$$CO_2 + H_2O \xrightarrow{\text{carbonic anhydrase}} H_2CO_3 \rightarrow H^+ + HCO_3^-$$

Since the protons secreted are, in fact, *generated* within the kidney, it is not the excretion of hydrogen ions by the kidney but rather the generation of bicarbonate which serves to offset the metabolic production of acid. Blood does not arrive at the kidney with "excess H^+" but rather with its bicarbonate content "depleted" and its buffers "acid loaded." For each millimole of hydrogen ion secreted, an equal quantity of bicarbonate is generated and exits across the basolateral membrane of the renal tubular cell to reenter the extracellular fluid. This bicarbonate restores the bicarbonate lost by titration of protons and "back titrates" buffers which have been titrated by acid,

$$HBuff + HCO_3^- \rightarrow Buff^- + H_2O + CO_2$$

Not all the bicarbonate generated by the kidney is generated by carbonic anhydrase. If you read on, you will see how a very important portion of renal bicarbonate generation is metabolically derived.

The hydrogen ion transport systems of the kidney vary in the different nephron segments.

The experimental techniques that have been most revealing in studying segmental hydrogen ion transport in the kidney are the following:

Tubular micropuncture This technique allows quantitative assessment of the transport of hydrogen ion and bicarbonate, in vivo, as the tubular fluid traverses nephron segments accessible to direct tubular puncture.

Tubule perfusion Utilizing micropuncture techniques, tubule segments, either in situ or isolated tubule segments dissected free of the kidney and bathed in a defined medium, can be studied.

Membrane vesicle preparations After homogenization, differential centrifugation can yield relatively pure samples of either apical or basolateral membrane. These membranes, under appropriate conditions, form vesicles whose internal and bathing media are defined by the experimental conditions. Studies of membrane vesicles have yielded valuable information about transport processes in the membranes of the renal tubule. Some membrane transport proteins have been isolated in sufficiently pure form to allow their incorporation into artificial vesicles (liposomes) allowing their biologic activities to be studied under even more fully defined conditions.

Patch clamping This technique measures the current carried by ions passing through the cell membrane. This technique has been applied to renal tubular cells to study the behavior of K^+ and Cl^- channels.

In the proximal tubule most of the hydrogen ion secretion is carried out by the sodium–hydrogen antiporter. A smaller fraction, about 35 percent, of proximal tubular hydrogen ion secretion is attributable to H^+-ATPase.

Hydrogen ion and bicarbonate are generated by the hydration of CO_2, catalyzed by intracellular carbonic anhydrase. The hydrogen ion is secreted into the tubular lumen in exchange for Na^+. The driving force for proton secretion by the $Na^+–H^+$ exchanger in the proximal convoluted tubule is the electrochemical gradient for sodium reabsorption across the apical (luminal) membrane, which results from the action of the $Na^+–K^+$ ATPase located on the basolateral (peritubular) membrane. Since $Na^+–H^+$ exchange is electroneutral, that is, a proton is transported out of the cell against the membrane potential gradient for each sodium ion which enters the cell along its electrical gradient, the net thermodynamic driving force for $Na^+–H^+$ exchange is the concentration gradient for sodium. The secretion of hydrogen ions across the apical membrane, into the tubular lumen, is mirrored by the transport of bicarbonate across the basolateral membrane into the peritubular space. As described previously (p. 41), in the proximal tubule most of the bicarbonate transport is carried out by a sodium-dependent cotransporter which transports sodium and bicarbonate in a ratio of 1:3, that is, $Na^+/3HCO_3^-$. The driving force for this electrogenic cotransporter is the electrochemical gradient favoring bicarbonate efflux. The transporter is inhibited by disulfonic stilbenes (SITS or DIDS).

Hydrogen ion secreted into the proximal tubular fluid titrates the filtered bicarbonate to form carbonic acid (H_2CO_3) which diffuses to the luminal membrane where membrane-bound carbonic anhydrase breaks down carbonic acid into CO_2 and H_2O. CO_2 diffuses into the cell. The net effect of proximal tubular hydrogen ion secretion is the "reabsorption" of approximately 85 percent of the filtered bicarbonate. On balance, the proximal tubule serves to replace bicarbonate which was lost by filtration at the glomerulus with bicarbonate generated by the secretion of H^+. The pH of tubular fluid close to the end of the proximal tubule is about 6.8. No "net secretion" of protons has occurred.

The rate of proximal tubular H^+ ion transport is regulated by several factors. As described earlier (pp. 37–38) the activity of the $Na^+–H^+$

antiporter is sensitive to activity changes in intracellular $[H^+]$; decreased intracellular pH stimulates antiporter activity. The "set point" for activation of the $Na^+–H^+$ exchanger varies with cell type. In skeletal and cardiac muscle, the exchanger is inactive at physiologic intracellular pH and is activated only when intracellular pH falls. In contrast, the renal proximal tubular brush border $Na^+–H^+$ exchanger has a set point which allows the exchanger to function at the resting pH of the proximal tubular cells and thereby to play an important role in renal hydrogen ion secretion. Cellular acidification, as a result of changes in systemic acid balance, stimulates $Na^+–H^+$ exchange.

Proximal tubular H^+ secretion via $Na^+–H^+$ exchange is also regulated by the availability of buffer, predominantly HCO_3^-, in proximal tubular fluid. Tubular fluid bicarbonate facilitates proximal tubular H^+ excretion in two (related) ways. First, by buffering secreted H^+, luminal bicarbonate prevents the buildup of a proton gradient which would limit $Na^+–H^+$ exchange. Second, luminal bicarbonate, reacting with secreted hydrogen ions, forms H_2CO_3 which is dehydrated to CO_2 and water by membrane-bound carbonic anhydrase. The diffusion of CO_2 into the proximal tubular cell results in intracellular acidification and stimulates the antiporter. The bicarbonate dependence of proximal $Na^+–H^+$ antiporter activity probably plays a role in the adaptation (i.e., increase) in proximal tubular bicarbonate reabsorption which characterizes both the "maintenance phase" of metabolic alkalosis and chronic respiratory acidosis (see pp. 82–83, 126–127).

Proximal tubular H^+ secretion is also regulated by peritubular factors. An increase in peritubular CO_2 tension leads to cellular acidification and stimulates H^+ secretion. Increased peritubular bicarbonate concentration, by limiting basolateral bicarbonate efflux, inhibits proximal tubular H^+ secretion.

In the distal convoluted tubule and collecting tubule, hydrogen ion secretion is accomplished almost exclusively by H^+-ATPase. The epithelium of the collecting tubules is made up of several distinct cell types. The proportions and transport properties of these cell types differ in the various collecting duct segments. The collecting tubule is considered to be made up of the cortical collecting tubule (CCT), medullary collecting tubule (MCT), and the papillary collecting tubule (PCT).

Intercalated cells, rich in cytosolic carbonic anhydrase, comprise 20 to 40 percent of the epithelial cells in the CCT and a smaller proportion of the surface epithelium in more distal segments. The intercalated cells transport hydrogen ions via H^+-ATPase. Principal cells, which reabsorb sodium and secrete potassium, do not appear to contain a proton-translocating ATPase or to transport hydrogen ions.

The intercalated cells of the *cortical* collecting tubule are adapted for either the secretion of hydrogen ion or the secretion of bicarbonate. Alpha-intercalated cells, designed for acid secretion, have a H^+-ATPase pump on their apical border and a Cl^-–HCO_3^- exchanger on the basolateral membrane. In beta-intercalated cells, specialized for bicarbonate secretion, the positions of the transport proteins are reversed. A H^+-ATPase is located on the basolateral membrane and a Cl^-–HCO_3^- exchanger on the luminal membrane.

The proton pumps of these two types of intercalated cell are related and both are classified as vacuolar H^+-ATPases but the Cl^-–HCO_3^- antiporters differ. The protein responsible for basolateral Cl^-–HCO_3^- exchange in alpha-intercalated cells appears to be very similar if not identical to the band 3 protein which makes up a large portion of red blood cell membrane protein. The Cl^-–HCO_3^- antiporter localized on the apical membrane of beta-intercalated cells appears to differ structurally. It does not react with monoclonal antibodies directed against either the red cell band 3 protein or the basolateral chloride–bicarbonate exchange protein. Unlike the basolateral chloride-bicarbonate exchanger, the apical Cl^-/HCO_3^- antiporter is not inhibited by SITS or DIDS. The function of the apical Cl^-/HCO_3^- antiporter appears to be to excrete bicarbonate under conditions of bicarbonate excess. It has been suggested that it might serve a role in chloride reabsorption, chloride exiting via chloride channels on the basolateral membrane.

The intercalated cells of the *medullary* collecting tubule and *papillary* collecting tubule are exclusively of the hydrogen ion secreting variety.

Recent evidence suggests the presence of another H^+ secretory transporter, H^+–K^+ ATPase, in the collecting tubule. This nonelectrogenic ATPase is responsible for H^+ secretion and K^+ reabsorption by the chief cells of the gastric mucosa. Energy (from the splitting of ATP) is required to move H^+ out of the cell and K^+ into the cell, both against electrochemical gradients. H^+-K^+ ATPase in connecting tubules, like that in the gastric mucosa, is inhibited by omeprazole and by the anion, vanadate.

Bicarbonate, generated by the secretion of protons across the apical membrane by H^+-ATPase in the collecting tubule, is transported out of the cell by a basolateral chloride-bicarbonate exchanger. The activities of these two transport proteins are closely linked: the activity of the apical transporter is probably rate-limiting.

Hydrogen ion secretion in the distal convoluted tubule and the various collecting duct segments is subject to regulation in response to the requirements for maintenance of systemic acid–base balance. As described earlier (p. 35) intracellular pH plays an important role in the regulation of H^+-ATPase activity by stimulating the fusion of subapical pump-bearing vesicles with the cell membrane, thereby increasing H^+ pump activity. Peritubular factors also regulate H^+-ATPase activity. As was the case for the Na^+-H^+ exchanger, peritubular CO_2 concentration regulates intracellular pH. Peritubular bicarbonate concentration modulates the exit of HCO_3^- at the basolateral membrane.

Hydrogen ion secretion into the tubular fluid in the collecting duct creates an electrochemical gradient which ultimately limits further H^+ secretion. Factors which dissipate the electrochemical gradient resulting from electrogenic H^+ ion secretion facilitate proton secretion. The active transport of hydrogen ions is often linked to the parallel transport of chloride ions through chloride channels. Chloride transport prevents the development of a potential difference and thereby facilitates proton secretion. This is clearly seen in the parietal cells of the gastric mucosa where active hydrogen ion secretion is associated with passive chloride secretion. The movement of chloride, through chloride channels, into lysosomal vesicles facilitates the acidification of the vesicle fluid by proton-translocating ATPase (H^+-ATPase.) Similarly, in the collecting duct, hydrogen ion secretion by H^+-ATPase is linked, in some manner, to the movement of chloride from cell to lumen through apical chloride channels. Hydrogen ion secretion may be regulated by the availability of chloride to prevent the buildup of a potential gradient as a result of electrogenic hydrogen ion secretion.

Buffering of secreted H^+ also facilitates proton secretion. In the collecting tubule, buffering is attributable to phosphate and other nonvolatile buffers since virtually all the filtered bicarbonate has been reabsorbed more proximally. Under special circumstances, the presence of nonreabsorbable anions, such as penicillin or para-aminohippurate, in the collecting duct tubular fluid may facilitate H^+ secretion by creating a favorable electrochemical gradient, that is, by rendering the lumen more electronegative and by combining with secreted hydrogen ions. Aldosterone actively stimulates hydrogen ion secretion in the collecting tubule. In part this is attributable to the action of aldosterone in stimulating sodium reabsorption and increasing the lumen-negative transmembrane potential difference. There is also evidence that aldosterone may stimulate hydrogen ion secretion via mechanisms which are independent of sodium transport.

In its overall role in maintaining systemic acid–base balance, the kidney must generate an amount of bicarbonate (or excrete a quantity of acid) which will match the daily net acid produced by metabolic processes. The kidney filters almost 4000 mmol of bicarbonate daily. About 85 percent of the bicarbonate lost by filtration at the glomerulus is replaced by bicarbonate generated by the secretion of H^+ ($Na^+–H^+$ exchange) in the proximal tubule. The secretion of H^+ which titrates bicarbonate in the filtrate is closely linked stoichiometrically with the reabsorption of filtered sodium. The remaining 15 percent (400–500 mmol) is removed from the tubular fluid before the fluid reaches the collecting tubule, that is, in the loop of Henle and distal convoluted tubule.

This poses a problem. The electrochemical gradient in the ascending limb—lumen positive—created by active chloride reabsorption in the segment does not favor H^+ secretion which appears to be mediated by both $Na^+–H^+$ exchange and H^+-ATPase. More importantly, hydrogen ion secretion and the generation of bicarbonate which must be reabsorbed across the basolateral membrane would lead to an increase in bicarbonate concentration in the medullary interstitium where the high concentration of solutes would favor the deposition of insoluble calcium carbonate salts. While bicarbonate is removed from the fluid traversing the loop of Henle, this is accomplished, at least in part, without hydrogen ion secretion. How bicarbonate can be removed from the tubular fluid without secreting H^+ is a fascinating story which will become clear when we talk about ammonia.

After the filtered bicarbonate is titrated ("reabsorbed") by H^+ secretion, further acid secretion generates "new bicarbonate," that is, bicarbonate which is available to replace extracellular fluid bicarbonate and back titrate nonbicarbonate buffers. In the distal nephron, when all the filtered bicarbonate has been removed, secreted acid combines with urinary buffers, predominantly phosphate.

Phosphate buffer has a pK of 6.8; at the pH of glomerular filtrate (7.4) most of the phosphate is in the form of the base (HPO_4^{-2}).

$$7.4 = 6.8 + \log \frac{HPO_4^{-2}}{H_2PO_4^{-}}$$

$$7.4 = 6.8 + \log \frac{4}{1} \qquad (\log 4 = 0.6)$$

Only 20 percent of the phosphate is in the "acid" form ($H_2PO_4^{-}$).

Hydrogen ion secreted in the proximal tubule reduces the pH of tubular fluid to about 6.8. At this pH,

$$6.8 = 6.8 + \log \frac{1}{1} \qquad (\log 1 = 0)$$

50 percent of the phosphate is in the acid form. Since daily phosphate excretion is about 30 mmol, acidification of phosphate buffer to 6.8 represents the excretion of about 15 mmol of H^+ (or the generation of 15 mmol of "new bicarbonate").

In the collecting tubule, urine pH can be reduced as low as 4.8. At this pH,

$$4.8 = 6.8 + \log \frac{1}{100} \qquad \left(\log \frac{1}{100} = -2 \right)$$

At this minimal urinary pH, 99 percent of the phosphate is in the acid form, that is, $H_2PO_4^{-}$ but since only 30 mmol of phosphate are excreted daily, the kidney cannot generate more than 30 mmol of "new bicarbonate" by the secretion of protons to acidify urinary buffers.

Here is where ammonia comes into the picture. More than 100 years ago, it was recognized that urinary ammonium excretion increased when mineral acids were fed to animals.

Subsequently it was recognized that the kidney metabolized amino acids, predominantly glutamine, to produce ammonia (NH_3) which appeared as ammonium (NH_4^+) in the urine. Most textbooks showed the overall reaction as

$$\text{Glutamine} \xrightarrow{\text{renal glutaminase}} NH_3 + CO_2 + H_2O$$

It was generally accepted that NH_3 entered the tubular lumen by nonionic diffusion through renal tubular cells.

NH_3 was viewed as a weak base, available to buffer H^+ in the tubular lumen.

$$NH_3 + H^+ \rightarrow NH_4^+$$

Combination of NH_3 with H^+ to form NH_4^+ was believed to "trap" ammonia in acid urine since the ionic species (NH_4^+) could not diffuse back out of the tubule.

This view of the role of ammonia in renal acid secretion has been modified in several important ways in recent years.

First, the pK of the NH_3/NH_4^+ system (8.89 at 37°C) dictates that at intracellular pH NH_3 cannot represent more than 1 percent of the total NH_3/NH_4^+.

Therefore, the equations describing ammoniagenesis are more correctly written as

$$\text{Glutamine} \xrightarrow{\text{renal glutaminase}} NH_4^+ + \text{glutamate}^-$$

and a second reaction,

$$\text{Glutamate}^- \xrightarrow{\text{glutamate dehydrogenase}} NH_4^+ + \alpha\text{-keto-glutarate}^-$$

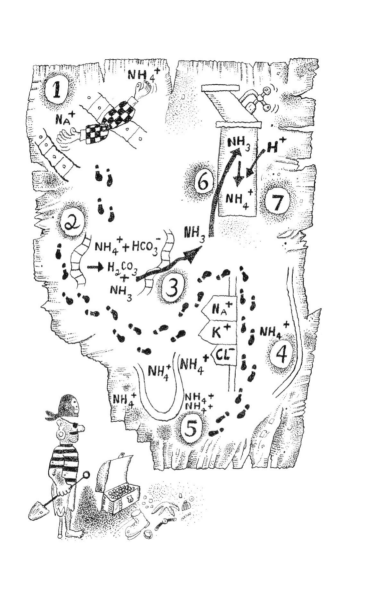

More important, it is now evident that NH_4^+ is actively secreted into the tubular fluid by several different renal tubular transport systems. It follows that urinary ammonium does not represent secreted hydrogen ion which has been buffered by NH_3 in the tubular fluid.

How does renal ammoniagenesis contribute to renal acid excretion? As outlined above, the breakdown of glutamine in the kidney, similar to gluconeogenesis in the liver (p. 49) yields both the weak acid, NH_4^+, and organic anions which can be oxidized to yield HCO_3^-. In the liver, both these products serve as substrates for urea production with the result that neither an acid nor a base are produced by hepatic gluconeogenesis.

In the kidney, however, NH_4^+ produced by the breakdown of glutamine is secreted into the tubular fluid and excreted in urine leaving behind organic anions which are metabolized to bicarbonate. This "new bicarbonate" is transported across the basolateral membrane to restore extracellular fluid and cellular buffers.

The path of ammonia through the kidney is interesting, involving several different renal transport systems. NH_4^+ is secreted into proximal tubular fluid, substituting for H^+, at the Na^+–H^+ exchanger (#1) (see "treasure map").

In the tubular fluid arriving at the loop of Henle, ammonium, a weak acid, titrates bicarbonate which escaped from the proximal tubule.

$$HN_4^+ + HCO_3^- \rightarrow NH_3 + H_2CO_3 \qquad (\#2)$$

H_2CO_3 is broken down to CO_2 and water in the early distal tubule after exposure to membrane-bound carbonic anhydrase and reabsorbed. This is the mechanism by which bicarbonate can be removed from the tubular fluid without secreting a hydrogen ion (see p. 58).

NH_3 diffuses into the medullary interstitium (#3) and NH_4^+ is actively transported into the medullary interstitium by the thick ascending limb, substituting for K^+ at the Na^+–K^+–$2Cl^-$ cotransporter (#4). Countercurrent multiplication creates a high concentration of NH_4^+ in the medulla (#5). The creation of a high concentration of NH_4^+ in the medullary interstitium, by active transport of NH_4^+ at the thick ascending limb and countercurrent multiplication, results in an increase in NH_3 (in equilibrium with NH_4^+). NH_3 diffuses into the collecting duct fluid where it is trapped as NH_4^+ by combining with (and buffering) H^+ secreted in the collecting tubule (#6).

In the overall balance since glutamine metabolism yields NH_4^+, the excretion of ammonium does not represent proton secretion (though protons are released and taken up along the way). The final step, NH_3 diffusion into the collecting tubule, and trapping of secreted H^+ to form NH_4^+ (#7) facilitates collecting tubule H^+ secretion. The net result is that glutamine metabolism by the kidney generates "new bicarbonate" from α-ketoglutarate in an amount equimolar with the ammonium which appears in the urine.

There is a parallelism between the two major mechanisms responsible for renal bicarbonate generation.

$$H_2CO_3 \rightarrow H^+ \text{ (secreted)} + HCO_3^- \text{ (reabsorbed)}$$

$$\text{Glutamine} \rightarrow NH_4^+ \text{ (secreted)} + \text{α-ketoglutarate}$$
$$\downarrow$$
$$HCO_3^- \text{ (reabsorbed)}$$

The unique feature of renal ammoniagenesis, which enables it to play a major role in the kidney's response to acid loading, is the provision of a base (NH_3) to serve as a proton acceptor. The dissociation of carbonic acid, like ammoniagenesis, provides a proton and a bicarbonate ion, but since there is no proton acceptor, proton secretion (and bicarbonate generation) are limited by buffer availability and hydrogen ion concentration gradients.

Since the titration of phosphate buffers can provide for only about 30 mmol of "new bicarbonate" production, renal ammoniagenesis represents an important contribution to the kidney's role in acid–base balance. When the kidney is required to excrete an acid load or generate an additional quantity of bicarbonate, this is accomplished by increased hepatic glutamine synthesis and increased renal ammoniagenesis. Ammonium excretion may be increased four- to fivefold in chronic metabolic acidosis.

In summary, H^+ ion is secreted by renal tubular epithelial cells, from the early proximal convoluted tubule to the proximal segments of the papillary collecting tubule. Hydrogen ion transport is achieved via specific transport proteins, the sodium–hydrogen antiporter and a H^+-ATPase pump. Most of the hydrogen ion secreted via Na^+–H^+ exchange in the proximal tubule generates bicarbonate to "replace" filtered bicarbonate; under normal conditions in man approximately 4500 mmol of bicarbonate are filtered daily. A small quantity of H^+, usually 50 to 80 mmol/day, secreted by H^+-ATPase in the distal nephron, results in urinary acidification and represents "new bicarbonate" generation which serves to offset metabolic acid production.

At first consideration this might seem an "energy inefficient" procedure for the maintenance of acid balance. Homer Smith wrote, "what engineer, wishing to regulate the composition of the internal environment of the body, on which the function of every bone, gland, muscle and nerve depends, would devise a scheme that operated by throwing the whole thing out sixteen times a day—and rely on grabbing from it as it fell to earth—only those precious elements which it wanted to keep?"

Consideration of the evolution of renal function from our early vertebrate ancestors yields some clues as to the "reason" for this seemingly inefficient process. Primitive fish such as the goose fish living in seawater, which is hypertonic relative to body fluids, have little need to secrete water. Sodium chloride, ingested while feeding, is actively secreted by specialized cells in the gill epithelium. The kidney consists of tubules only; glomeruli are rudimentary or absent altogether. The tubules actively secrete waste products and ingested toxins—largely organic acids. A small quantity of water diffuses into the tubule lumen along an osmotic gradient, forming urine. A kidney whose function is dependent on tubular secretion appears well suited to the marine environment.

Freshwater fish have glomerular kidneys. In freshwater fish, homeostasis and cell volume regulation require the excretion of water. Given the need to excrete a quantity of solute-free water, it is thermodynamically much more efficient to begin with a glomerular ultrafiltrate generated by the residual hydrostatic energy from the heart's pumping action and to reabsorb *millimolar* quantities of solute against relatively small solute concentration (activity) gradients leaving water to exit through water-impermeable segments of the distal nephron, than to actively transport (i.e., secrete) *molar* quantities of water. When fish migrate from freshwater into seawater, the glomeruli are seen to atrophy, glomerular filtration declines, and renal function is largely attributable to tubular secretion.

The tubules expend energy (derived from the enzymatic hydrolysis of ATP) to create an electrochemical gradient which facilitates the reabsorption of filtered sodium and chloride. This same gradient, without additional energy expenditure, provides the driving force for $Na^+–H^+$ exchange which mediates most of the generation of bicarbonate to replace filtered bicarbonate buffer ("replaced bicarbonate").

It seems likely that this renal tubular hydrogen ion transport process (proximal $Na^+–H^+$ exchange) which exchanges secreted protons for filtered sodium (bicarbonate) evolved as an accommodation to the need for solute and water homeostasis incurred when vertebrates ventured into freshwater or onto dry land, rather than as a system designed to meet a requirement for acid base homeostasis.

10

Clinical Disorders of Acid–Base Balance

In previous chapters it was argued that the wide variety of intracellular processes which are affected by hydrogen ion concentration mandate very high biologic priority for the maintenance of intracellular hydrogen ion concentration. Although many cells retain the ability to transport protons by Na^+–H^+ exchange or proton pumps (H^+-ATPase), with the evolution of the extracellular fluid as the "internal bathing compartment" for cells, the maintenance of cellular pH came to be dependent on the maintenance of the pH of the extracellular fluid. This dependence on extracellular fluid pH is probably best explained by effects of extracellular fluid hydrogen ion concentration and pCO_2 on proton entry into cells and limits imposed on membrane transport processes which move acid out of (or bicarbonate into) cells.

While cell function is probably most importantly related to intracellular pH, the extracellular fluid both mirrors and affects intracellular hydrogen ion concentration. As a consequence, disorders of acid–base balance can generally be analyzed in relation to the maintenance of extracellular (i.e., plasma) fluid pH.

Buffering and compensatory changes in acid excretion generally serve to maintain the hydrogen ion concentration of the extracellular fluid within a very narrow range, 36 to 44 nmol/L (pH = 7.36–7.40). When hydrogen ion concentration is increased beyond the normal limit, *acidemia* is said to exist. When hydrogen ion concentration is decreased below the normal limit, *alkalemia* is said to exist. Disorders which disturb acid–base balance and lead to acidemia or alkalemia may be recognized while the hydrogen ion concentration (i.e., pH) is still within the normal range. The term *acidosis* is applied when acid excretion is impaired (or base is lost) and *alkalosis* is used to denote conditions in which acid excretion or loss is excessive (or base added).

Acidosis or alkalosis without deviation of hydrogen ion concentration beyond the normal range is observed in several clinical states:

1. When the acid–base disorder is mild, hydrogen ion concentration may be deviated but still lie within the normal range, for example, $[H^+]$ may increase from 36 to 44 nmol/L in mild acidosis or decrease from 44 to 36 nmol/L in mild alkalosis.
2. When buffering is adequate to maintain $[H^+]$ within the normal range.
3. When compensatory hydrogen ion transport processes offset the initial acid–base disturbance so as to maintain $[H^+]$.
4. When there are two or more coexisting acid–base abnormalities, that is, mixed acidosis and alkalosis, there are offsetting effects on $[H^+]$; more about this later.

All extracellular buffers participate in the buffering of hydrogen ion. For each buffer pair (HCO_3^-/H_2CO_3, $HPO_4^{-2}/H_2PO_4^-$, protein$^-$/ protein-H^+, hemoglobin$^-$/hemoglobin-H^+) the ratio of buffer$^-$ ("the conjugate base") to buffer-H^+ ("the conjugate acid") and a constant (the equilibrium constant or pK) define the free hydrogen ion concentration. Measurement of the ratio of the conjugate base to the conjugate acid for any buffer pair, together with the pK of the buffer, allows calculation of the hydrogen ion concentration, the *isohydric principle*. In evaluating clinical disorders of acid–base balance, however, measurements of the components of the bicarbonate buffer system of extracellular fluid, that is, plasma, are particularly useful. This is so because

1. The components of the H_2CO_3/bicarbonate system are easily measured by standard clinical assays. The concentration of H_2CO_3 is directly proportional to the quantity of dissolved CO_2, which is a function of the partial pressure of CO_2 in blood. This is readily measured with a CO_2-sensitive electrode. Total CO_2, which includes both bicarbonate and dissolved CO_2, can also be determined by acidification of the blood and measurement of the CO_2 evolved. Since dissolved CO_2 normally constitutes

less than 5 percent of the total, it is often ignored and measurement of total CO_2 is used to estimate the concentration of bicarbonate.

2. The $H_2CO_3^-$ system is quantitatively the most important extracellular buffer system. While hydrogen ions are buffered by all the extracellular fluid and intracellular buffers, the H_2CO_3/HCO_3^- system exhibits two unique features—one is *biochemical*, the other *physiologic*.

First, let's consider the biochemical feature. The bicarbonate buffering system is an "open system." Unlike other buffer systems in which the addition of hydrogen ion, by combining with the conjugate base, increases the concentration of the conjugate acid, in the "open" bicarbonate system, buffering of protons results in the loss of conjugate base while the concentration of the conjugate acid (H_2CO_3) remains unchanged.

The plasma concentration of the conjugate acid of the system, H_2CO_3, is directly proportional to the concentration of dissolved CO_2 which, in turn, is determined by the partial pressure of CO_2 (pCO_2) in blood . Alveolar ventilation serves to maintain plasma pCO_2 within a fairly narrow range; in normal man this is close to 40 mmHg. When H_2CO_3 is formed by bicarbonate buffering of H^+,

$$H^+ + HCO_3^- \rightarrow H_2CO_3$$

the evolved H_2CO_3 increases the partial pressure of dissolved CO_2

$$H_2CO_3 \rightarrow CO_2 + H_2O$$

As a passive consequence of the increased CO_2 content of plasma arriving at the lung, the alveolar concentration of CO_2 is increased and more CO_2 is eliminated by respiration. The high degree of diffusibility of CO_2 and the high rate of blood flow through alveolar capillaries allow the pulmonary removal of excess CO_2 with little or no measureable increase in pCO_2. The importance of the difference between "closed" and "open" buffering can be seen in the following example:

The Henderson–Hasselbalch equation states

$$pH = pK + \log \frac{[base]}{[acid]}$$

For the bicarbonate buffer system at normal plasma pH,

$$7.4 = 6.1 + \log \frac{[\text{bicarbonate}]}{[H_2CO_3]}$$

Since the concentration of H_2CO_3 is directly related to $PaCO_2$ (the partial pressure of CO_2 in arterial blood), the term $0.03 \times PaCO_2$, can be substituted for $[H_2CO_3]$. (The solubility of CO_2 in plasma at body temperature is 0.03 mmol/liter/mmHg.) Inserting normal values,

$$7.4 = 6.1 + \log \frac{24\,\text{mmol/L}}{1.2\,\text{mmol/L}}$$

(The log of 20 = 1.3.)

If we were to add 5 mmol of a strong acid (i.e., 5 mmol of H^+) to 1 liter of plasma, neglecting other buffers, 5 mmol of HCO_3^- would be converted to H_2CO_3. The new ratio of base/acid would be $(24 - 5)/(1.2 + 5) = 3.06$. Since the log of 3.06 = 0.48, the pH would decrease from 7.4 to 6.58 (corresponding to a hydrogen ion concentration of 257 nM).

However, in the "open" bicarbonate buffer system $PaCO_2$ (and therefore H_2CO_3) remains unchanged. With the addition of 5 mmol of H^+, bicarbonate is again decreased from 24 to 19 mmol/L but as the concentration of H_2CO_3 is unchanged, the base/acid ratio becomes 19/1.2 = 15.8. Since the log of 15.8 = 1.2, pH decreases from 7.4 to 7.3 (corresponding to an increase in hydrogen ion concentration from 40 nmol/L to 50 nmol/L).

The "open" buffer system thereby permits the addition of 5,000,000 nmol of H^+ with only a 10 nmol/L increase in hydrogen ion concentration; 99.998 percent of the added hydrogen ion is buffered. The buffering capacity of the "open" system is twenty times greater than that for a "closed" bicarbonate buffer system.

This is considered a "biochemical" feature of the bicarbonate buffering system since the same reaction, that is, the titration of bicarbonate with unchanged $PaCO_2$, would occur if acid were added to an open beaker containing bicarbonate in solution.

A second, *physiologic*, feature of the plasma bicarbonate buffer system makes it uniquely suited to the regulation of acid–base balance. Perturbations in extracellular fluid hydrogen ion concentration result in changes in alveolar ventilation and the pulmonary excretion of CO_2 and in the renal generation of HCO_3^-; these compensatory pulmonary and renal responses tend to correct or minimize the deviations in both components of the bicarbonate buffer system. Unlike other extracellular or intracellular buffer systems, the concentration of either component of the bicarbonate buffer pair can be increased or decreased in response to acid–base disturbances; the changes in $PaCO_2$ and bicarbonate concentration provide a physiologic amplification of the buffering capacity of the bicarbonate system.

3. Finally, because the lung and the kidney directly control the concentration of the conjugate acid (H_2CO_3) and conjugate base (HCO_3^-), measurements of this buffer pair provide a conceptual framework for the classification and understanding of the pathogenesis of acid–base disorders.

According to this schema, acid–base disorders are classified as either *respiratory* or *metabolic* in origin (Fig. 4).

Respiratory acid–base disorders arise from changes in the efficiency of removal of CO_2 by the lungs. Changes in $PaCO_2$ and the consequent changes in the concentration of H_2CO_3 in plasma are responsible for changes in H^+ concentration in respiratory acidosis and alkalosis. When alveolar ventilation or pulmonary gas exchange are impaired and $PaCO_2$ increases, the concentration of H_2CO_3 in plasma increases. Respiratory acidosis results from the dissociation of H_2CO_3 to yield H^+. Conversely, alveolar hyperventilation results in reduced $PaCO_2$ and decreased plasma concentration of H_2CO_3; as a consequence, $[H^+]$ is reduced resulting in respiratory alkalosis.

Metabolic acid–base disorders arise when the titration of cellular and extracellular buffers by protons generated by metabolism (or gained or lost via the gastrointestinal tract) is not precisely balanced by renal bicarbonate generation. When acid production exceeds renal bicarbonate generation, plasma bicarbonate falls and $[H^+]$ is increased. This is termed "metabolic acidosis" although we recognize that it may result equally from the metabolic overproduction of protons, the loss of base

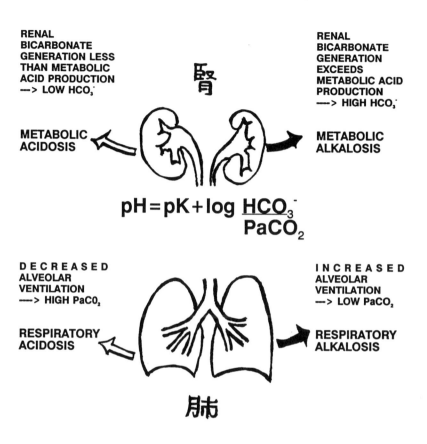

RENAL
BICARBONATE
GENERATION LESS
THAN METABOLIC
ACID PRODUCTION
—> LOW HCO₃⁻

METABOLIC
ACIDOSIS

RENAL
BICARBONATE
GENERATION
EXCEEDS
METABOLIC ACID
PRODUCTION
—> HIGH HCO₃⁻

METABOLIC
ALKALOSIS

$$pH = pK + log \frac{HCO_3^-}{PaCO_2}$$

DECREASED
ALVEOLAR
VENTILATION
—> HIGH PaCO₂

RESPIRATORY
ACIDOSIS

INCREASED
ALVEOLAR
VENTILATION
—> LOW PaCO₂

RESPIRATORY
ALKALOSIS

Fig. 4. The Yin and Yang of Acid–Base Disorders.

from the gastrointestinal tract, or the failure of the kidney to excrete protons, that is, to regenerate bicarbonate. Conversely, metabolic alkalosis results when renal bicarbonate generation or base intake exceeds the production of acid (protons) by metabolic processes; plasma bicarbonate concentration increases and $[H^+]$ falls.

Each of these four primary disorders is characterized by a deviation in hydrogen ion concentration. The deviations in hydrogen ion concentration are offset (to a variable degree) by immediate buffering by extracellular fluid buffers and intracellular buffers.

The buffer composition of extracellular and intracellular fluids differ considerably. In the extracellular fluid, buffering is largely attributable to weak acids and bases—the predominant buffer is the H_2CO_3/HCO_3^- system [whose capacity is greatly enhanced by the maintenance of a near constant $PaCO_2$ (H_2CO_3)]; additional buffering is attributable to phosphates and weak organic acids. Protein concentration, averaging 7 g/dl, contributes little to buffering of extracellular fluid.

In contrast, intracellular fluid buffering is largely attributable to protein. Intracellular fluid bicarbonate concentration (at $pH_i = 7$) is only 10 mmol/L and phosphate concentration is low. Protein concentration is about 20 g/dl in intracellular fluid and more than 30 g/dl in the erythrocyte. Intracellular buffering results from the binding of protons to, or release of protons from, carboxyl groups or amide groups whose pK is between 6 and 8. The buffering power of cellular proteins is large (48 to 60 slykes). *Slykes* are units of buffering capacity, defined as the quantity (mmoles) of acid or base required to produce a shift of 1 pH unit/L. The name derives from Donald van Slyke, one of the pioneer physiologic chemists in the first quarter of the twentieth century.

The relative contributions of extracellular and intracellular buffering to acid–base homeostasis are not clearly established and are probably not the same for all acid–base disturbances. Let's begin by considering respiratory acid–base disorders.

Respiratory acid–base disorders are due to changes in the concentration of CO_2, which is freely diffusible across cell membranes. Experimentally, hypercapnea and hypocapnea are readily produced by changing the composition of inspired air. Changes in CO_2 concentration in plasma present increased or decreased acid loads to the cell. Increased $PaCO_2$ results in greater diffusion of CO_2 into cells and the generation of protons (by the dissociation of H_2CO_3). Conversely, decreased $PaCO_2$ leads to a loss of intracellular CO_2 and a decrease in $[H^+]$. Bicarbonate, the major extracellular fluid buffer, is ineffective in buffering protons derived from H_2CO_3 since the reaction

$$CO_2 + H_2O \rightleftharpoons H_2CO_3 \rightleftharpoons H^+ + HCO_3^-$$

is shifted to the right ($\rightarrow$) as $PaCO_2$ is increased. The only available buffers for H^+ generated from CO_2 are the small amounts of extracellular and intracellular nonbicarbonate inorganic buffers and the large pool of intracellular protein buffers. Intracellular buffers account for most of the buffering in respiratory acid–base disorders. Protons generated by the dissociation of H_2CO_3 are buffered by imidazole groups and other bases with appropriate pK and bicarbonate is transported into the extracellular fluid. This process mimics that which occurs as erythrocytes take up CO_2 produced in tissues and generate bicarbonate which enters the plasma.

The remarkably efficient erythrocyte anion exchanger (band 3 protein) appears to be a specialized form of a chloride/bicarbonate exchanger present in the membrane of most, if not all, cells. It is likely that chloride/bicarbonate exchange plays an important role in cellular buffering of CO_2 in states of respiratory acidosis or alkalosis. This exchanger, facilitating HCO_3^- efflux, functions to prevent an accumulation of bicarbonate when $PaCO_2$ is increased, and intracellular H_2CO_3 dissociates to yield H^+ and HCO_3^-. Conversely, the exchanger operating in the reverse direction (i.e., bicarbonate influx) maintains intracellular bicarbonate concentration when $PaCO_2$ is reduced.

The experimental means for studying the relative contributions of extracellular fluid and intracellular fluid buffering in metabolic acidosis or alkalosis have traditionally entailed addition of either acids or bases *to the extracellular fluid*. The contribution of blood and extracellular fluid buffers can be estimated by measurement of the change in bicarbonate concentration and calculation of the quantity of hydrogen ion bound to nonbicarbonate buffers. The contribution of buffering by cellular buffers (and bone) is calculated as the difference between the quantity of protons administered and that which can be accounted for in the extracellular fluids. The results of such studies have suggested that the intracellular and extracellular buffers serve, in some more or less coordinated manner, to buffer acid or base loads. With mineral acid (e.g., dilute hydrochloric acid) loading, it is estimated that 40 to 50 percent of the added protons are buffered in the extracellular fluid. The remainder of buffering is attributed to cellular buffers and, possibly, to buffering by bone minerals. I find this conclusion surprising since consideration of the importance of intracellular pH would dictate that cellular buffering should primarily serve the role of maintaining a near constant intracellular hydrogen ion concentration and might be expected to be called into play when cells are challenged by acute increases or decreases in proton concentration *within* the cell.

How can the findings of these classic studies of acid loading be reconciled with the intuitive notion that intracellular buffering should be reserved for perturbations in intracellular hydrogen ion concentration?

Protons, as strong (mineral) or weak (organic) acid, added to the extracellular fluid are rapidly buffered by bicarbonate and other extracellular buffers. This buffering results in a fall in extracellular fluid bicarbonate concentration. This might be expected to result in the transport of bicarbonate out of the cell into the extracellular fluid. The cell membrane is an effective barrier to the passive diffusion of either protons or bicarbonate into or out of cells. Does the bicarbonate/chloride exchanger, or the $Na^+/3HCO_3^-$ cotransporter provide a mechanism to explain the changes in intracellular buffer composition in *metabolic* acid–base disorders? Since the chemical concentration gradient for bicarbonate provides the driving force and is the critical determinant of the *direction* of bicarbonate transport for both these transporters, it can be hypothesized that when extracellular buffering in metabolic acidosis results in a fall in bicarbonate concentration, cellular bicarbonate efflux might result. Within the cell this would shift the equilibrium,

$$H_2CO_3 \rightarrow HCO_3^- + H^+$$

yielding H^+, which would be buffered by protein buffers, and bicarbonate, which would replace that lost by bicarbonate efflux.

Conversely, when extracellular fluid (ECF) bicarbonate concentration is increased (metabolic alkalosis), the anion exchanger or Na/HCO_3^- cotransporter might function to facilitate bicarbonate influx. This would shift the H_2CO_3/bicarbonate equilibrium ($H_2CO_3 \leftarrow HCO_3^- + H^+$) and cause dissociation of H^+ from protein buffers.

When one estimates the distribution of an acid or base load between extracellular and cellular buffers by the "book-keeping method" described earlier, it may appear that both buffer systems share in the disposition of proton or base load, but *conceptually* it seems more consistent with the notion of defense of intracellular pH to view the changes in H^+ buffering by cellular protein buffers as a consequence of stabilizing intracellular $[HCO_3^-]$ and $[H^+]$.

Following the immediate defense of tissue and extracellular fluid hydrogen ion concentration by cellular and extracellular buffering, a *biochemical effect* which can be observed in vitro, *physiologic changes* serve to further restore pH toward normal. In each of the four major classes of acid–base disorder the physiologic or "compensatory" changes serve to restore the ratio of HCO_3^-/H_2CO_3 toward normal. Since all extracellular buffer systems are interrelated (the isohydric principle) changes in the ratio of HCO_3^-/H_2CO_3 are accompanied by a parallel rectification of all other buffer ratios. These "compensatory responses" are best examined in chronic acid–base disturbances in which a new steady state is attained.

In respiratory acidosis and respiratory alkalosis the primary deviation in hydrogen ion concentration results from a new steady-state concentration of CO_2 in blood, either an increased or decreased $PaCO_2$. The physiologic compensatory change which follows the primary respiratory disturbance is a change in renal acid excretion.

In chronic respiratory acidosis, in response to the primary increase in $PaCO_2$, plasma bicarbonate concentration increases. The ratio $[HCO_3^-]/PaCO_2$ increases and pH is restored towards normal.

How does the increase in bicarbonate come about?

In part, the increased $PaCO_2$ results directly in increased bicarbonate generation through the chemical reaction:

$$CO_2 + H_2O \rightleftharpoons H_2CO_3 \rightleftharpoons H^+ + HCO_3^-$$

When CO_2 diffuses into cells and is hydrated to H_2CO_3 and dissociates, the generated H^+ is buffered by intracellular buffers. The bicarbonate is transported into the extracellular fluid. Plasma bicarbonate concentration increases by about 1 mEq/L for each 10-mmHg increment in $PaCO_2$.

The kidney is responsible for the "physiologic" compensatory increase in bicarbonate concentration. Renal acid excretion, that is, bicarbonate generation, increases. Renal ammoniagenesis is stimulated and collecting tubule H^+-ATPase activity is stimulated by the increase in $[H^+]$ or $PaCO_2$. Under normal acid–base conditions, an increase in plasma bicarbonate concentration would lead to an increased filtered load of bicarbonate and result in prompt excretion of the added bicarbonate, that is, the bicarbonate "threshold" would be exceeded. In chronic respiratory acidosis, however, the renal threshold for bicarbonate, a proximal tubular function, is increased. Proximal tubular bicarbonate reabsorption is mediated by $Na^+–H^+$ exchange. Studies of vesicles derived from renal proximal tubule brush border membranes reveal an increase in the number of $Na^+–H^+$ antiporters in rabbits with chronic respiratory acidosis. Basolateral membrane vesicles demonstrate increased $Na^+–3HCO_3^-$ cotransport. Such findings give evidence that the adaptation to chronic respiratory acidosis is mediated, in part, by a change in the number or activity of membrane transport proteins. As described earlier (p. 36), sodium–hydrogen antiporter activity is very sensitive to pH; increased $[H^+]$ could account for the increase in proximal tubule bicarbonate threshold. It seems more likely, however, that increased $PaCO_2$ rather than increased $[H^+]$ is responsible for the increased proximal tubular Na–H exchange and bicarbonate threshold since a similar increase in bicarbonate threshold is observed in chronic metabolic alkalosis (i.e., when $[H^+]$ is decreased). Once serum bicarbonate concentration increases, increased proximal tubular fluid bicarbonate concentration facilitates sodium–hydrogen exchange by providing a source of buffer in the lumen and by removing secreted hydrogen ion,

$$H^+ \text{ (secreted)} + HCO_3^- \text{ (in lumen)} \rightarrow H_2CO_3 \rightarrow CO_2 + H_2O$$

The presence of carbonic anhydrase at the luminal membrane of the proximal tubule catalyzes the dehydration of H_2CO_3 to CO_2 and water and prevents an accumulation of H^+.

In chronic respiratory alkalosis, the primary decrease in $PaCO_2$ is offset by a decrease in plasma bicarbonate concentration. The ratio of $HCO_3^-/PaCO_2$ and pH are restored toward normal.

What is the mechanism responsible for the decrease in plasma bicarbonate?

The "acute biochemical effect," the consumption of bicarbonate,

$$HCO_3^- + H^+ \rightarrow H_2CO_3 \rightarrow CO_2 + H_2O$$

accounts for a small decline in plasma bicarbonate concentration, averaging about 2 mEq/L for each 10 mmHg decrement in $PaCO_2$.

The decrease in plasma bicarbonate appears to be due to both an increase in metabolic acid production (lactic acid, see p. 129) and a decrease in proximal tubular bicarbonate reabsorption. Decreased pCO_2 might account for reduced sodium–hydrogen antiporter activity and decreased renal threshold for bicarbonate. Vesicle studies suggest a decrease in basolateral membrane $Na^+/3HCO_3^-$ transport in chronic respiratory alkalosis.

The important role of the kidney in compensating for primary respiratory acid–base disorders by resetting plasma bicarbonate concentration is mirrored by the role of the lung in compensating for primary metabolic acid–base disorders (the Yin and Yang concept).

Chronic metabolic acidosis is most commonly observed in advanced renal failure. Renal acid excretion in the "new steady state" that characterizes very slowly progressive renal failure is thought to closely approximate metabolic acid production. There may, in fact, be a small steady accumulation of H^+ (positive acid balance) which is neutralized or titrated by crystalline calcium carbonate in bone.

The physiologic compensation which allows the kidney, with its much reduced number of nephron units, to maintain net acid secretion will be discussed in a later section (pp. 96–97).

Decreased plasma bicarbonate concentration, the consequence of buffering of hydrogen ions in chronic metabolic acidosis, is offset by a decrease in $PaCO_2$ and H_2CO_3. The physiologic compensation, increased alveolar ventilation, results from the stimulatory effect of increased plasma or cerebrospinal fluid $[H^+]$ on medullary chemoreceptors which control the rate and depth of respiration.

Conversely, in chronic metabolic alkalosis, increased plasma bicarbonate concentration is offset by a decrease in alveolar ventilation and consequent increase in $PaCO_2$.

How well these compensatory mechanisms serve to correct the extracellular fluid pH in chronic acid–base disorders differs depending on which acid–base disorder you look at. In most instances, plasma pH is not returned fully to normal. The important point is that we judge the degree to which compensatory responses—either pulmonary or renal—have restored hydrogen ion concentration toward normal as being "appropriate" or "inappropriate" by comparing the observed pH, $PaCO_2$, and plasma bicarbonate with values observed in patients who have what appear to be "pure" forms of each of these acid–base disorders. When the compensatory response deviates significantly from that predicted based on empiric observations, it is taken as evidence of a second acid–base disturbance—a "mixed acid–base disorder."

The basic principle is as follows:

In *metabolic* disorders, primary deviations in plasma bicarbonate concentration and pH elicit compensatory changes in alveolar ventilation and $PaCO_2$. The magnitude of the observed change in $PaCO_2$, in relation to the deviation in plasma bicarbonate concentration, is used to assess the respiratory response to metabolic acid–base disorders.

In *respiratory* disorders, primary deviations in $PaCO_2$ and pH elicit compensatory changes in renal bicarbonate generation and plasma bicarbonate concentration. The magnitude of the observed

(Continued)

change in plasma bicarbonate concentration, in relation to the deviation in $PaCO_2$, is used to assess the compensatory metabolic response to respiratory acid–base disorders.

In *metabolic acidosis,* hydrogen ion excess results in titration of cellular and extracellular buffers; plasma bicarbonate concentration is decreased. The fall in pH of plasma perfusing the brainstem, and carotid and aortic bodies leads to increased respiration and alveolar ventilation. The resultant fall in $PaCO_2$ shifts the ratio of $HCO_3{}^-/PaCO_2$ (and all other buffer systems) toward normal. The expected degree of respiratory compensation (fall in $PaCO_2$), as judged from data obtained in patients with "uncomplicated" metabolic acidosis, is given by the relation,

$$\triangle PaCO_2 = 1.0 \text{ to } 1.3 \, (\triangle HCO_3{}^-)$$

This can be seen graphically in Figure 5.

If the decrement in $PaCO_2$ significantly exceeds that predicted from this relationship, it suggests an additional stimulus for hyperventilation, that is, a *superimposed respiratory alkalosis.* Conversely, if the decrement in $PaCO_2$ is significantly less than that predicted, a *superimposed respiratory acidosis* is presumed to exist.

In *metabolic alkalosis,* increased plasma pH leads to a reduced rate of respiration and alveolar ventilation. The consequent increase in $PaCO_2$ shifts the buffer ratio and pH toward normal. The equation,

$$\triangle PaCO_2 = 0.7 \, (\triangle HCO_3{}^-)$$

describes the predicted change in $PaCO_2$ for a given increase in plasma bicarbonate concentration.

Values of $\triangle PaCO_2$ greater or smaller than predicted from this relationship suggest a superimposed (or concurrent) respiratory disorder. If the increase in $PaCO_2$ is less than predicted, a combined metabolic alkalosis and *respiratory alkalosis* is suggested. If the increment in $PaCO_2$ is greater than that predicted, a combined metabolic alkalosis and *respiratory acidosis* is likely.

Similarly, we can utilize empiric observation to provide data on the

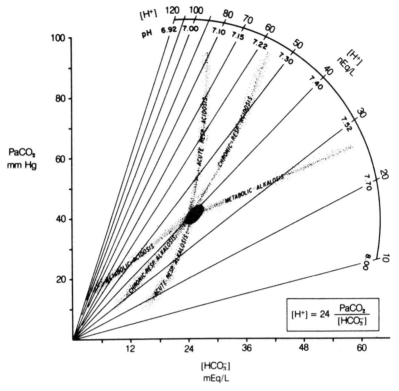

Fig. 5. Acid–base template. The Henderson equation, shown in the box at the lower right, relates hydrogen ion concentration, $[H^+]$ to the ratio of $PaCO_2$ and $[HCO_3^-]$. The shaded zones indicate the expected relationship between $PaCO_2$ and $[HCO_3^-]$ in uncomplicated or single acid–base disturbances. Values which fall outside the shaded zones suggest the presence of mixed acid–base disorder. (From J. J. Cohen and J. P. Kassirer, *Acid/Base,* Little, Brown and Company, 1982.)

magnitude of expected change in serum bicarbonate for a given change in $PaCO_2$ in *respiratory* acid–base disorders. The expected changes are quite different in acute and chronic respiratory disorders.

Why is chronicity a consideration in respiratory acid–base disorders, but not metabolic acidosis or alkalosis?

The lung removes more than 10 mmol of CO_2 *each minute* as compared with the kidney which normally excretes 50 to 100 mmol of acid *per day*. Clearly an increase or decrease in alveolar ventilation can produce a large change in $PaCO_2$, and therefore pH, within minutes. The kidneys respond to signals (change in either H^+ or $PaCO_2$) rapidly, but 24 to 48 hours are usually required before the change in renal acid excretion and bicarbonate generation is appreciated as a significant change in plasma bicarbonate concentration.

In chronic *respiratory acidosis*, the increased $PaCO_2$ and reduced pH stimulate renal bicarbonate generation. The expected increase in serum bicarbonate is given by the relation,

$$\triangle HCO_3^- = 0.35\,(\triangle PaCO_2)$$

An increase in bicarbonate concentration greater than that predicted suggests a coexisting *metabolic alkalosis*; an increase in bicarbonate less than predicted is taken as evidence of a coexisting *metabolic acidosis*.

In chronic *respiratory alkalosis*, the expected fall in plasma bicarbonate is given by the relation,

$$\triangle HCO_3^- = 0.4 \text{ to } 0.5\,(\triangle PaCO_2)$$

Changes in plasma bicarbonate concentration greater than or less than predicted are taken as evidence of coexisting *metabolic acidosis* or *metabolic alkalosis*, respectively.

What happens to acid production and excretion in these compensated acid–base states?

Compensated acid–base disorders are characterized by changes in both bicarbonate concentration and $PaCO_2$ with a ratio of base/acid near normal, and consequently near normal pH, in the extracellular fluid. In the new steady state the overall balance of both volatile and nonvolatile acids is maintained. The excretion of CO_2 by the lungs and the generation of bicarbonate by the kidneys are regulated normally and respond appropriately to acute acid or base loading despite large deviations in the components of the bicarbonate buffer system.

This may seem surprising but some musing about the garfish and the Himalayan Sherpa should remind us that it is quite natural. In fish, oxygen and CO_2 exchange occur across the gill epithelium. Oxygen is considerably less soluble in water than CO_2; a high rate of water flow across the gill surface is required to achieve the required oxygen uptake by the gill epithelium. The resultant removal of CO_2 accounts for the maintenance of the plasma concentration of CO_2 ($PaCO_2$) in the range of 2 to 4 mmHg. As the pH of blood in fish is typically about 7.5, serum bicarbonate concentration is similarly quite low, as compared with vertebrates, averaging 3 to 6 mmol/L. The garfish, *Lepisosteus*, which is related to the lungfish, is a gill breather in the winter, but in the summer when there is less oxygen dissolved in water, the garfish relies on primitive lungs for breathing. In winter, the garfish has a $PaCO_2$ of 3 to 4 mmHg and plasma bicarbonate of 6 to 7 mmol/L. In the summer, when the garfish becomes an air breather, $PaCO_2$ increases to 13 mmHg and plasma bicarbonate to 10 mmol/L. Day-to-day regulation of acid–base balance is apparently maintained despite this marked change in the ratio, $HCO_3{}^-/PaCO_2$, in what might be considered a form of "warm weather compensated respiratory acidosis."

At the other extreme, Himalayan Sherpas (as an example of adapted residents of high altitudes) have both reduced $PaCO_2$ (20 mmHg) and plasma bicarbonate (14 mmHg). Despite this chronic respiratory alkalosis, day-to-day acid balance is maintained without the need to invoke unique physiologic mechanisms.

An interesting aspect of acid–base regulation in these various sustained, compensated acid–base disorders is the apparent dissociation of *net acid secretion*—that component of renal hydrogen ion secretion and bicarbonate generation which balances daily metabolic acid production (and a small quantity of gastrointestinal loss of base)—and the *bulk of renal hydrogen ion secretion* which serves to replace bicarbonate filtered by the kidney. Since virtually all filtered bicarbonate is "reabsorbed" or "replaced," the total quantity of hydrogen ion secreted in "reabsorbing" bicarbonate is directly related to the filtered load which is a function of the glomerular filtration rate and the plasma bicarbonate concentration.

As pointed out earlier, under normal acid–base conditions (plasma bicarbonate 25 mEq/L) about 4500 mEq of bicarbonate are filtered and reabsorbed daily. When plasma bicarbonate concentration is elevated, for example, to 40 mEq/L as in chronic respiratory acidosis or chronic metabolic alkalosis, the daily filtered load of bicarbonate (neglecting changes in glomerular filtration rate) may increase to 7200 mEq; virtually all this bicarbonate is "reabsorbed" by proximal hydrogen ion secretion via Na^+–H^+ exchange. Conversely, when plasma bicarbonate is reduced, for example, to 15 mEq/L as in chronic metabolic acidosis or chronic respiratory alkalosis, the daily filtered load of bicarbonate falls to 2700 mEq. Despite the very great range of hydrogen ion secretion subserving the function of bicarbonate reabsorption or replacement, *net acid excretion*, averaging 50 to 100 mEq daily, remains closely geared to metabolic acid production in all these acid–base states. The ability of the kidney to respond to these quantitatively disparate requirements is best understood if we consider bicarbonate reabsorption and net acid excretion as separate and distinct regulated systems.

Though admittedly an oversimplification, bicarbonate reabsorption is predominately a proximal tubular process, mediated by Na^+–H^+ exchange and controlled, in large measure, by $PaCO_2$. In each of the four classes of acid–base disorder, bicarbonate reabsorption varies directly with $PaCO_2$ and bears no constant relation to plasma hydrogen ion concentration (Table 10.1).

Table 10.1 Regulation of Bicarbonate Reabsorption

	Bicarbonate Reabsorption	$PaCO_2$	$[H^+]$
Metabolic acidosis	↓	↓	↑
Metabolic alkalosis	↑	↑	↓
Respiratory acidosis	↑	↑	↑
Respiratory alkalosis	↓	↓	↓

CO_2, freely diffusible into renal tubular cells and rapidly hydrated to H_2CO_3, provides both the source of secreted hydrogen ion and the stimulus for Na^+–H^+ antiporter activity.

While hydrogen ion secretion and bicarbonate reabsorption are conventionally considered important components of renal acid–base regulation, it should be recognized that in the proximal tubule

1. Hydrogen ion, though *secreted*, is not *excreted* (hydrogen ion combines with tubular fluid bicarbonate).
2. Bicarbonate is not *reabsorbed* (H_2CO_3 formed in the tubular fluid is dehydrated and CO_2 diffuses across the tubular membrane).
3. The quantity of hydrogen ion secreted into the proximal tubule (as indicated in Table 10.1) is unrelated to the systemic hydrogen ion concentration.

Conceptually, proximal tubular hydrogen ion secretion—mediated by the Na^+–H^+ antiporter—appears more intimately related to the maintenance of sodium balance than to acid–base homeostasis. The following argument may clarify this seemingly radical suggestion. There is little or no *direct* reabsorption of bicarbonate in the proximal tubule; in the absence of secreted hydrogen ion, bicarbonate can be considered a nonreabsorbable anion. The ability to modulate sodium reabsorption in the proximal tubule, normally about 80 to 85 percent of the filtered load, would be severely limited if it were not for the Na^+–H^+ exchange mechanism which assures almost complete reabsorption of filtered bicarbonate. Failure to "reabsorb" filtered bicarbonate in the proximal tubule results in both metabolic acidosis and substantial loss of filtered sodium. In acid–base disorders with varying plasma bicarbonate concentration, Na^+–H^+ exchange facilitates the maintenance of a constant fractional sodium reabsorption in the face of wide variations in the anion composition of the glomerular filtrate.

Net acid excretion, the quantity of acid excreted (or bicarbonate generated) to offset metabolic acid production, can best be equated with H^+ secretion by H^+-ATPase in the collecting tubules and with the renal excretion of ammonium. These two processes, each resulting in bicarbonate generation, appear exquisitely sensitive to acute changes in acid load, whether exogenous or endogenous. It is likely that the stimulus for changes in renal net acid excretion is the extracellular fluid hydrogen ion concentration but it is not yet clear whether the effects of H^+ are directly on H^+-ATPase and renal tubular enzymes responsible for glutamine breakdown or are mediated by some messenger or cell-signaling system. The suggestion that proximal tubular hydrogen ion secretion primarily serves the requirement for sodium reabsorption while distal tubular and collecting tubule acid secretion serves the needs of acid–base homeostasis appears to be supported by the finding that the two proximal tubular hydrogen ion transport mechanisms (Na^+–H^+ exchanger and the $Na^+/3HCO_3^-$ cotransporter) are both sodium-dependent while the hydrogen ion transport systems in the collecting tubule (H^+-ATPase and Cl^-/HCO_3^-) are sodium-independent.

If the compensatory changes in ventilation and renal bicarbonate generation are sufficient to result in proportionate changes of $PaCO_2$ and HCO_3^-, and pH maintained in the normal range, how can one tell whether the patient has a compensated acidosis or a compensated alkalosis? Suppose that you are on 42nd Street and 6th Avenue and I ask you to meet me at the NYU Medical Center, which is at 31st Street and 1st Avenue. You could come south to 31st Street, then east or... you could go east to 1st Avenue, then south... or could follow a zig-zag pattern. How would I know which way you came? Well, I might see you walking along before you arrive... most acid–base compensations are not "complete." Or, you might tell me what you saw along the way... that's what the patient tells us. We'll discuss this in the next chapter.

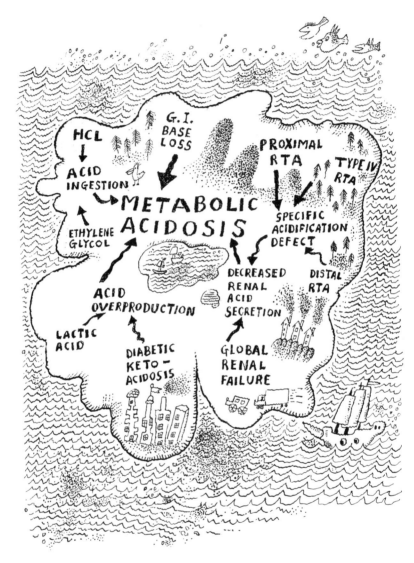

11

Metabolic Acidosis: A Bird's Eye View

In general terms, metabolic acidosis results when renal acid excretion is reduced, when metabolic acid production is increased, when acid is ingested, or when base is lost from the body.

The kidney is the sole organ which normally secretes acid to offset metabolic acid production and gastrointestinal base loss.

Acid is excreted by the kidney by three different renal tubular processes:

1. Hydrogen ion is secreted by H^+-ATPase on the apical membrane of intercalated cells of the collecting tubule. Bicarbonate, generated by the dissociation of H_2CO_3 or the hydroxylation of CO_2, is actively transported across the basolateral membrane by a chloride-bicarbonate exchanger.
2. Hydrogen ion is secreted by a sodium–hydrogen antiporter on the apical membrane of proximal tubular cells. Bicarbonate generated by the dissociation of H_2CO_3 is actively transported across the basolateral membrane by a sodium-bicarbonate cotransporter.
3. Hydrogen ion, combined with ammonia as NH_4^+, is generated from glutamine by glutaminase I and glutamic dehydrogenase in proximal tubular cells and is secreted into the lumen. Alpha-ketoglutarate, the other product of ammoniagenesis, is metabolized to bicarbonate and transported across the basolateral cell membrane.

In each of these processes, it should be recognized, although we conventionally refer to acid excretion or secretion, the common feature is bicarbonate generation; the hydrogen ion or ammonium ion which appears in the urine may be viewed as the byproduct of bicarbonate generation by the renal tubule.

You might ask, aren't "hydrogen ion secretion" and "bicarbonate generation" really two sides of the same coin? Why do you try to distinguish between them?

The same phenomenon may be viewed in different ways, which seem to be "two sides of the same coin." For the purpose of understanding renal acidification and systemic acid–base balance "hydrogen ion secretion" and "bicarbonate generation" are interchangeable. However, if we consider that the hydrogen ion and the bicarbonate ion are not always derived from the same process (i.e., the dissociation of H_2CO_3) and that proton transport and bicarbonate transport are performed by different transport proteins, it should be clear that the idea that these are "two sides of the same coin" is more apparent than real. In some circumstances this difference, which appears to be "a point of view," may be fundamentally important. For 1000 years Ptolemaic astronomy provided a satisfying and basically accurate description of the motions of heavenly bodies and the question whether the earth or the sun was the center of the universe might have been dismissed as a trivial issue or a "point of view." Clearly the predictions of Ptolemy and Copernicus would not serve today's space travellers equally well! Similarly, the difference between "hydrogen ion secretion" and "bicarbonate generation" may assume greater importance when we have a clearer understanding of how the generation or transport of protons or bicarbonate is selectively changed by disease and when we can affect these processes by pharmacologic means.

Bicarbonate, generated by these tubular transport processes, serves several functions. Bicarbonate generated in the proximal tubule replaces, mole for mole, the bicarbonate removed from plasma by glomerular filtration. Bicarbonate generated in the collecting tubule segments and bicarbonate generated from α-ketoglutarate (sometimes termed "new bicarbonate," though from the foregoing it should be clear that all the generated bicarbonate is "new") serves to replace bicarbonate lost in buffering protons generated by metabolism, to back titrate nonbicarbonate buffers, and to replace bicarbonate (or bicarbonate "equivalents") lost through the gastrointestinal tract.

Impaired Renal Acid Excretion

Metabolic acidosis, attributable to a specific disorder of any of the three major tubular transport systems responsible for bicarbonate generation, is termed *renal tubular acidosis* (RTA).

Distal or type I renal tubular acidosis is the result of impaired hydrogen ion secretion in the cortical and medullary collecting tubules. In these tubular segments, hydrogen ion secretion is mediated by H^+-ATPase localized in intercalated cells. Proton secretion by H^+-ATPase is electrogenic, that is, it generates a lumen-positive transepithelial voltage. In the cortical collecting tubule, proton secretion is facilitated by active (electrogenic) sodium reabsorption which creates a net lumen-negative driving force for active proton secretion. H^+ secretion in the medullary collecting tubule is sodium-independent.

H^+-ATPase (proton-translocating ATPase) is capable of actively transporting protons against a steep electrochemical gradient. Since virtually all the filtered bicarbonate has already been titrated in more proximal segments, hydrogen ion secreted in the collecting duct segments titrates urinary buffers—predominately phosphate. The pK of the $HPO_4^{-2}/H_2PO_4^-$ buffer pair is 6.8; phosphate exerts its maximal buffering in the pH range 7.8 to 5.8. As urinary pH is reduced further, by hydrogen ion secretion, a significant transmembrane H^+ concentration gradient, approaching 1000:1 (i.e., 3 log orders) is created. The epithelium of the collecting tubule is relatively "tight," that is, hydrogen ions do not readily diffuse back across the luminal membrane despite the marked H^+ gradient created by active H^+ secretion.

Impaired distal (i.e., collecting tubule) acidification results from a defect in the ability of the hydrogen ion transport system to create or to maintain the steep H^+ gradient which characterizes maximal urinary acidification. Urine pH in "classic" or distal RTA is usually not below 6 to 7 despite systemic acidemia.

In the most common form of distal RTA (idiopathic distal RTA), the defect in collecting tubule hydrogen ion transport appears to be an impaired *rate* of proton pumping. The mechanism for this "rate-limited" defect in hydrogen ion transport is not known.

Impaired distal acidification and distal RTA is also seen during treatment with several different drugs. The fungal antibiotic, amphotericin, renders the apical membrane "leaky" and permits the back diffusion of hydrogen ion from the tubular lumen. Lithium and amiloride, by blocking sodium reabsorption, decrease lumen electronegativity in the cortical collecting tubule and thereby increase the electrochemical gradient against which the proton-translocating ATPase pump must operate. A similar defect in distal renal acidification has been described in obstructive uropathy. The finding of distal RTA associated with a defect in gastric acid secretion, as an endemic disorder in Thailand, suggests a possible environmental inhibitor of H^+-K^+ ATPase may be responsible.

As described earlier (p. 59) the failure to maximally acidify the urine reduces net renal acid excretion (i.e., bicarbonate generation) by 20 to 30 mmol H^+ daily. This represents the difference between the amount of acid carried by urinary buffers at the pH of late proximal tubular fluid (pH = 6.8) and that of urine at a pH of 4.8. The urinary excretion of ammonium is decreased as less NH_3 (which diffuses into the lumen from the interstitium) is trapped in the collecting tubule. Ammonium, generated by the proximal tubule, which is not excreted in the urine, is returned to the renal venous blood and is utilized by the liver in urea synthesis. In this process a proton is generated, thereby offsetting the bicarbonate generated by renal ammoniagenesis. Impaired secretion of hydrogen ion by the collecting tubule results in the urinary loss of sodium and potassium since phosphate excretion obligates cation excretion. The loss of sodium, albeit small, results in aldosterone overproduction and mineralocorticoid probably contributes to the potassium loss and hypokalemia which characterize type I RTA.

The defect in distal nephron acid secretion results in a positive acid balance requiring a fraction of daily metabolic acid production to be neutralized by body buffers.

> How does plasma bicarbonate reach a steady state or plateau if metabolic acid production exceeds net renal acid excretion?

There is one source of buffer that we have not considered yet. The skeleton is made up of an organic phase (ground substance, collagen, and cells) and a mineral phase consisting of crystalline lattices of calcium, phosphate and hydroxyl ions (hydroxyapatite), calcium phosphate (brushite), and calcium carbonate. The surface of bone is negatively charged and normally binds sodium and potassium ions. Protons, from extracellular fluid, exchange for surface-bound sodium and potassium in acute metabolic acidosis.

In chronic metabolic acidosis, bone serves as a large reservoir of buffer to neutralize the small but unremitting positive balance of hydrogen ions. This buffering is in part physicochemical, a direct chemical reaction between protons and the most labile pool in bone, calcium carbonate. Hydrogen ions combine with carbonate,

$$2H^+ + CO_3^{-2} \rightarrow H_2CO_3$$

and the calcium ion is released into the extracellular fluid. The physicochemical buffering of hydrogen ions by bone is very much the same as the buffering of excreted metabolic acids by coral in a marine fish tank in that it mantains $[H^+]$ in the face of positive acid balance.

The titration of acid by bone leads to the slow dissolution of bone. Bone growth in children with renal tubular acidosis may be retarded. The release of calcium from bone, together with the alkaline pH in distal tubular fluid, leads to the precipitation of calcium salts and medullary nephrocalcinosis.

Patients with type I (distal) RTA may at times present with severe metabolic acidosis and hypokalemia requiring emergency treatment with intravenous sodium bicarbonate and potassium. More commonly the major clinical manifestations of distal RTA are related to the long-standing mild metabolic acidosis and potassium loss. Most patients with distal RTA require chronic therapy with sodium bicarbonate or a base equivalent such as sodium citrate or acetate. Since the quantity of bicarbonate normally generated by distal tubular acid secretion and renal ammoniagenesis is relatively small, that is, about the same order of magnitude as daily metabolic acid production (1 mEq/kg body wt), the treatment of distal RTA requires the administration of only 40 to 60 mEq of bicarbonate daily. This is usually effective in preventing the bone complications seen in long-standing RTA.

Impaired hydrogen ion secretion in the proximal tubule causes a form of renal tubular acidosis termed *type II-RTA*. As described in earlier sections (p. 69), hydrogen ion secretion mediated by Na^+-H^+ exchange in the proximal convoluted tubule and early portions of the distal convoluted tubule serves to titrate filtered bicarbonate and facilitates sodium reabsorption in these tubular segments. Impairment in hydrogen ion secretion in type II RTA is usually accompanied by defects in other proximal tubular transport functions. The tubular reabsorption of glucose, uric acid, phosphate, and amino acids is often impaired; the complex of tubular transport defects is termed the Fanconi syndrome.

The cause of proximal RTA is not known. Administration of acetazolamide or other inhibitors of carbonic anhydrase reduce proximal tubular bicarbonate reabsorption and result in metabolic acidosis, mimicking proximal RTA, but there is no evidence that carbonic anhydrase deficiency is responsible for type II RTA. Proximal RTA and the Fanconi syndrome have been reported in a variety of disorders characterized by proximal renal tubular injury. The causes of proximal RTA fall into two broad categories: injury secondary to tubular toxins such as streptozotocin, outdated tetracycline, and maleic acid and injury secondary to the deposition of heavy metals (lead poisoning, Wilson's disease), crystals (cystinosis, tyrosinemia), or proteins (multiple myeloma, light-chain deposit disease).

The defect in proximal H^+ secretion in proximal RTA or in patients receiving an inhibitor of carbonic anhydrase results in the delivery of a large fraction, often 15 to 20 percent, of the filtered bicarbonate to the distal nephron. The intact distal hydrogen secretory transport processes, while able to transport H^+ against a steep electrochemical gradient, have a limited capacity. Bicarbonate, which escapes reabsorption in the proximal tubule, exceeds the distal hydrogen ion secretory capacity; bicarbonate is lost into the urine. The urine becomes alkaline despite maximal distal hydrogen ion secretion. The loss of bicarbonate in the urine and the titration of bicarbonate stores by metabolic acid production are not matched by renal bicarbonate generation; plasma bicarbonate concentration falls. As plasma bicarbonate concentration decreases, the filtered load of bicarbonate presented to the proximal tubule declines to a level at which the reduced proximal proton secretion is sufficient to titrate most of the filtered bicarbonate. At this point, generally when plasma bicarbonate concentration has declined to approximately 15 mEq/L, the intact distal hydrogen ion secretion is unmasked; the urine is again rendered free of bicarbonate and urine pH is reduced. A new steady state is attained; distal hydrogen ion secretion (and ammoniagenesis) replaces the bicarbonate titrated by metabolic acid production and plasma bicarbonate concentration stabilizes.

Proximal RTA is often mild and usually does not require treatment. If proximal tubule bicarbonate loss is not severe, distal hydrogen ion secretion may be adequate to maintain net acid excretion equal to metabolic acid production. When the proximal defect is severe, bicarbonate loss in the urine may be profound and replacement of base is necessary. Patients with proximal RTA may require as much as 5 to 15 mmol/kg body weight of bicarbonate to partially correct the metabolic acidosis. Attempts to replace bicarbonate loss by administration of sodium bicarbonate lead to prompt increase in distal bicarbonate delivery and further bicarbonaturia. The delivery of filtered sodium and bicarbonate to the distal tubule and collecting duct, together with the stimulus for sodium reabsorption provided by aldosterone, creates a greater lumen-negative potential which favors potassium secretion. Hypokalemia is common in proximal RTA and is often accentuated by sodium bicarbonate administration which increases urinary bicarbonate loss.

The third form of renal tubular acidosis, type IV RTA, includes several closely related disorders in which the common features are impaired bicarbonate generation, metabolic acidosis, and hyperkalemia. In type IV RTA, the major defect in renal acidification is attributable to impaired renal ammoniagenesis. Inhibition of renal glutaminase activity is responsible for impaired renal ammoniagenesis.

The most common cause of type IV RTA is a selective deficiency in aldosterone production. This is frequently associated with reduced plasma renin activity and angiotensin II concentration; angiotensin II is an important regulator of adrenal aldosterone synthesis. This disorder, hyporeninemic hypoaldosteronism, is most commonly observed in adult-onset diabetics with modest reduction in glomerular filtration. Aldosterone deficiency contributes to metabolic acidosis in several ways. First, and probably most importantly, aldosterone deficiency results in hyperkalemia which inhibits renal glutaminase activity and limits renal ammonigenesis. Hyperkalemia may inhibit ammonium reabsorption through the $Na^+/K^+/Cl^-$ triple transporter at the loop of Henle and disrupt the generation of a medullary concentration gradient for ammonia.

Further, aldosterone deficiency, by reducing principal cell sodium absorption, limits the generation of a lumen-negative driving force for proton secretion. Aldosterone deficiency probably has a direct effect on α-intercalated cells reducing H^+-ATPase activity. In type IV RTA associated with aldosterone deficiency, urinary acidification is modestly impaired but the urine pH can be reduced below 5.5.

Hyperkalemic RTA is also observed following urinary tract obstruction, in patients with sickle cell disease, and associated with administration of amiloride. The common feature is probably a defect in the generation of lumen-negative potential in the cortical collecting tubule. Amiloride directly blocks apical membrane sodium channels. Tubular obstruction and sickle hemoglobinopathy may impair sodium transport in this segment. As a consequence, proton and potassium secretion are impaired. The urine cannot be acidified below pH 5.5. Patients with these forms of type IV RTA usually have normal or elevated plasma aldosterone concentration and may be considered "aldosterone resistant." They differ from patients, usually children, with specific end-organ resistance to aldosterone.

Urinary bicarbonate loss is not a prominent feature of type IV RTA and, since the defect in acid excretion is distal, the metabolic acidosis is usually not severe. Treatment in patients with type IV RTA is directed mainly at correction of the hyperkalemia. Patients who are deficient in aldosterone may respond to the chronic administration of a synthetic mineralocorticoid such as fludrocortisone. Patients with decreased sensitivity to aldosterone are more effectively treated by the chronic administration of thiazide diuretics or furosemide which promote potassium excretion. The importance of hyperkalemia in the pathogenesis of metabolic acidosis in type IV RTA is demonstrated by the observation that correction of hyperkalemia with the ion exchange resin, sodium polystyrene sulfonate (Kayexalate), leads to correction of metabolic acidosis.

Each of the forms of renal tubular acidosis is characterized by both a defect in hydrogen ion secretion and a tendency to lose sodium. In proximal (type II) RTA, sodium loss accompanies bicarbonaturia. In distal (type I) RTA and type IV RTA sodium loss is associated with failure to secrete protons and, in the case of type IV, a voltage-dependent defect attributable to aldosterone deficiency. The urinary loss of sodium stimulates sodium retention in the proximal and distal nephron. Impaired H^+ secretion in the proximal tubule and collecting tubule render bicarbonate a poorly reabsorbable ion. Sodium reabsorption is therefore limited by chloride availability. As a consequence, chloride reabsorption increases. The loss of filtered bicarbonate and the increase in chloride reabsorption result in *hyperchloremic metabolic acidosis*. By this we mean that the fall in plasma bicarbonate concentration, with renal tubular acidosis, is mirrored by an increase in plasma chloride concentration.

We are ready now to consider the form of metabolic acidosis, uremic acidosis, seen with advanced renal disease and reduced glomerular filtration. The kidney displays a remarkable ability to maintain the overall balance of water, sodium, potassium, and hydrogen ion despite reduction in the rate of glomerular filtration to less than 25 percent of normal.

Having stressed the role of the renal tubule in hydrogen ion secretion and bicarbonate generation, it may seem surprising to relate uremic acidosis to the glomerular filtration rate (GFR). While renal tubular acid secretion is relatively independent of the rate of glomerular filtration, in progressive renal parenchymal disease, the decrease in glomerular filtration rate provides a rough estimate of the loss of overall renal mass, that is, the number of nephrons lost as a result of scarring and atrophy. Some of the features of uremic acidosis are related to the marked reduction in glomerular filtration, rather than decreased hydrogen ion transport per se.

Metabolic acidosis, though present when GFR is only modestly reduced (about 50 percent), is usually mild until the glomerular filtration rate falls to about 10 percent of normal. Hydrogen ion secretion by the collecting tubules of residual functioning nephrons increases strikingly; titratable acid (a measure of total hydrogen ion secreted in the distal nephron segments) is not markedly different from that in normals. The increase in acid secretion per residual nephron reflects the stimulatory effect of metabolic acidosis on collecting duct hydrogen ion secretion.

Increased glomerular filtration rate in residual hypertrophied nephrons (increased single-nephron GFR) results in an increased filtered load of phosphate per nephron. Parathyroid hormone, secreted in excess in renal failure, inhibits proximal tubular reabsorption of phosphate and provides for the delivery of an increased quantity of phosphate buffer to the collecting tubule. The increased delivery of buffer facilitates proton secretion.

Renal ammoniagenesis is stimulated by metabolic acidosis. Single-nephron ammonia production may increase as a consequence of hypertrophy of residual nephrons but total renal ammonia production and renal ammonium secretion are decreased when nephron number is markedly decreased. Disruption of the medullary countercurrent gradient for ammonium may contribute to decreased secretion of ammonia into the collecting tubule. Decreased bicarbonate generation by ammoniagenesis is quantitatively the major factor in the genesis of uremic metabolic acidosis.

Proximal tubular bicarbonate wasting—as seen in type II RTA—may contribute to uremic acidosis. In general, the pH of the urine is acid, that is, about 5.0, but may increase, with bicarbonaturia, when the plasma bicarbonate concentration is increased by sodium bicarbonate infusion or bicarbonate ingestion. This "bicarbonate wasting" may reflect decreased proximal tubular hydrogen ion secretion, attributable to the inhibitory effect of parathyroid hormone on Na^+-H^+ antiporter activity. Alternatively, hyperfiltration in residual nephrons may result in a single-nephron filtered load of bicarbonate which exceeds the proximal tubular hydrogen ion secretory capacity.

In summary, the pathogenesis of uremic metabolic acidosis includes several defects. With nephron loss, total hydrogen ion secretion and bicarbonate generation by the collecting tubules is moderately decreased (despite considerable increase in acid secretion per residual tubule). In some instances, proximal tubule bicarbonate wasting contributes to metabolic acidosis. Renal ammoniagenesis and urinary ammonium excretion are reduced. Net renal acid secretion, the sum of hydrogen ion secreted by the collecting tubule in titrating urinary buffers (mainly phosphate) and urinary ammonium (representing the quantity of bicarbonate generated by renal ammoniagenesis), usually falls short of metabolic acid production by only 10 to 20 mEq daily. The "short fall" in net acid excretion is largely attributable to impaired ammoniagenesis.

The protons generated by metabolic processes in excess of renal net acid secretion are buffered by extracellular, intracellular, and bone buffers. The buffering of hydrogen ion by bone is facilitated by the increase in parathyroid hormone, secondary hyperparathyroidism, in renal failure. Parathyroid hormone promotes the cell-mediated resorption of bone and release of phosphate and carbonate buffer by stimulating bone-reabsorbing cells, osteoclasts.

In the course of progressive renal failure mild metabolic acidosis becomes evident when glomerular filtration rate is only moderately reduced. In the early stage of renal failure, as net acid excretion fails to match the rate of metabolic acid production, plasma bicarbonate concentration is mildly decreased and, as in renal tubular acidosis, hyperchloremia is present. With progression of renal disease, metabolic acidosis worsens and bicarbonate concentration is further decreased. Anions, such as sulfate, phosphate, and organic acids, whose excretion depends on glomerular filtration, accumulate in the plasma and account for an increased anion gap.

In renal tubular acidosis, decreased plasma bicarbonate concentration is matched by increased chloride concentration and the anion gap is unchanged. We describe this as a *normal anion gap, hyperchloremic metabolic acidosis*.

In uremic acidosis, with marked reduction in glomerular filtration, the increased plasma concentration of sulfate, phosphate, and some organic acids causes an *increased anion gap*. This is termed an *increased*

A Short Discourse on the "Anion Gap"

You know that the sum of cations and anions in any solution must be equal. There are many substances in plasma which are either anions or cations at the usual pH of plasma. Quantitatively, the predominant cations are sodium and potassium. The major anions are chloride and bicarbonate. For many years these were the only ions readily measured in clinical laboratories. Other anions and cations were referred to as "unmeasured." The "anion gap" refers to the numerical difference between the sum of "measured anions" and "measured cations."

Because potassium concentration represents only a small fraction of total cations, it is often omitted from the equation (i.e., it is considered an unmeasured cation).

$$\text{Anion gap} = [Na^+] - ([Cl^-] + [HCO_3^-])$$

Normally, the anion gap is about $12\,\text{mEq/L}$ [i.e., $140 - (104 + 24)\,\text{mEq/L}$].

Since the total anions must equal the total cations, the anion gap is apparent, not real. Therefore,

$$Na^+ + \text{"unmeasured cations"}$$

$$= Cl^- + HCO_3^- + \text{"unmeasured anions"}$$

The true relationship which defines the anion gap is

$$\text{Anion gap} = [Na^+] - ([Cl^-] + [HCO_3^-])$$

$$= \text{"unmeasured anions"} - \text{"unmeasured cations"}$$

The "unmeasured cations" (which are today routinely measured in clinical laboratories) are K^+, Mg^{2+}, and Ca^{2+} accounting for about $10\,\text{mEq/L}$. Hydrogen ion (in nanomolar concentration in plasma) is not reflected in the calculation of the anion gap. The "unmeasured anions," totaling approximately 22 mEq/L, consist of phosphate, sulfate, organic acids (about 6 mEq/L), and proteins (about 16 mEq/L).

An increase in "anion gap" reflects either an increase of unmeasured anions or a decrease in unmeasured cations. In patients with metabolic acidosis, the most frequent cause of increased anion gap is an increase in unmeasured anions, either anions such as sulfate or phosphate, which accumulate when glomerular filtration is impaired, or organic acids which are produced in excess.

anion gap, normochloremic metabolic acidosis. While decreased filtration and excretion of metabolic acids with "unmeasured anions" accounts for the increased anion gap in uremia, the metabolic acidosis in uremia is caused by decreased renal tubular acid secretion and renal ammonia-genesis (i.e., bicarbonate generation). In this respect uremic acidosis shares many of the transport defects which characterize renal tubular acidosis.

Lactic Acid Overproduction

Let's look at some forms of metabolic acidosis that are caused by metabolic overproduction of acid. Lactic acidosis is a potentially lethal form of metabolic acidosis which results from a breakdown in mito-chondrial energy transfer. The anaerobic phase of glucose metabolism (the glycolytic or Embden–Meyerhof cycle) generates energy, in the form of two ATP molecules, and results in the formation of two molecules of pyruvate for each molecule of glucose consumed. This is accomplished by a series of phosphorylations; the conversion of fructose-6-phosphate to fructose-1,6-diphosphate, catalyzed by 6-phosphofructokinase, is the rate-limiting reaction. This series of reactions takes place in the cytosol. A key enzymatic step in the glycolytic pathway, the oxidation of glyceraldehyde-3-phosphate to pyruvate, requires the oxidized form of nicotinamide adenine dinucleotide (NAD^+), which is converted to the

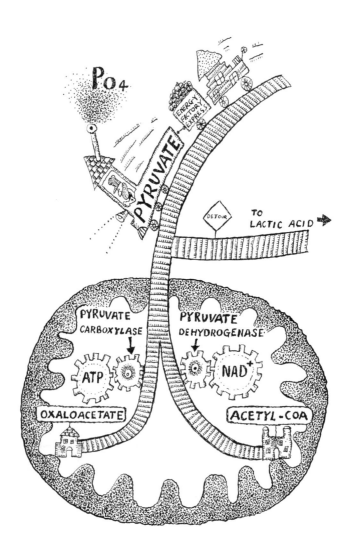

reduced form, NADH.

$$\text{Glyceraldehyde-3-Phos} + NAD^+ \rightarrow \text{pyruvate} + NADH$$

For glycolysis to proceed, NAD^+ must be continuously regenerated. When oxygen and metabolic substrates are abundant and mitochondrial oxidative metabolism is intact, NAD^+ is regenerated from NADH within the mitochondrion. The ratio $[NADH]/[NAD^+]$, the redox (REDuction OXidation) potential, reflects the relative rates of NAD^+ consumption in the cytosol and NAD^+ regeneration by mitochondrial oxidation.

Pyruvate, generated by glycolysis, is readily converted to lactate, a reaction catalyzed by lactate dehydrogenase (LDH). The reaction serves to regenerate an equimolar quantity of NAD^+.

$$\text{Pyruvate}^- + NADH + H^+ \xrightarrow{\text{LDH}} \text{lactate}^- + NAD^+$$

Rearranging this equation,

$$\frac{[\text{Lactate}^-]}{[\text{Pyruvate}^-]} = kEq \times \frac{[NADH]}{[NAD^+]} \times [H^+]$$

makes it apparent that the ratio of the concentration of lactate to pyruvate is determined by the ratio $[NADH]/[NAD^+]$ and the concentration of hydrogen ion. Under normal conditions the ratio lactate/pyruvate $= \frac{10}{1}$ and the overall reaction describing glycolysis may therefore be written as

$$C_6H_{12}O_6 \rightarrow 2CH_3^-CH(OH)COO^- + 2H^+$$

glucose   lactate

It is estimated that under basal condition 1000 to 1700 mmol of lactate and hydrogen ion are generated daily by this pathway. Clearly cellular buffering could not neutralize this massive proton load. Both the generated lactate and the protons are normally consumed by mitochondrial metabolism. Pyruvate is transported across the inner membrane of the mitochondria by a specific anion transporter, in exchange for phosphate. It does not apppear that lactate can be actively transported across the inner mitochondrial membrane. The metabolism of pyruvate in the mitochondrial matrix shifts the equilibrium between lactate and pyruvate, toward pyruvate,

$$NAD^+ + lactate^- \xrightarrow{LDH} pyruvate^- + NADH + H^+$$

and leads to consumption of lactate produced by glycolysis.

Following mitochondrial uptake, pyruvate is metabolized via two rate-limiting unidirectional reactions. Pyruvate is converted to oxaloacetate (catalyzed by pyruvate carboxylase) and to acetyl CoA (catalyzed by pyruvate dehydrogenase). The pyruvate carboxylate pathway leads ultimately to the resynthesis of glucose and requires ATP. The pyruvate dehydrogenase pathway, leading to the oxidation of two-carbon fragments to CO_2 and water, requires NAD^+. The metabolism of pyruvate is therefore critically dependent on the availability of both NAD^+ and ATP in the mitochondrial matrix. The regeneration of NAD^+ and the synthesis of ATP, from ADP, in the mitochondrium is dependent on the oxidation of organic substrates. Specific transporters in the mitochondrial membrane facilitate the entry of organic anions such as malate, glutamate, and α-ketoglutarate. Oxidation of these substrates provides the energy for the regeneration of NAD^+ from NADH and for the extrusion of protons from the mitochondrial matrix. The electrochemical proton gradient (protonmotive force) so created drives H^+ ions back across the mitochondrial membrane via the H^+-ATPase or as it functions in this setting, ATP synthase, resulting in ATP generation. This is the process, referred to earlier (p. 35), by which proton transport serves to generate ATP.

When mitochondrial energy coupling is defective, the reduced availability of NAD^+ and ATP inhibit pyruvate utilization. But energy (ATP) production from glucose does not cease. The rate-limiting enzyme in the glycolytic pathway, 6-phosphofructokinase, is stimulated by the reduced concentration of ATP (or the increased ratio ADP/ATP) resulting in acceleration of anaerobic glycolysis. While this provides continued ATP production, the "cost" of the energy is high. Increased generation of pyruvate via glycolysis, together with impaired mitochondrial pyruvate utilization and a higher ratio $NADH/NAD^+$, results in lactic acid overproduction. The accumulation of lactate and protons in lactic acidosis can be seen as a consequence of both the overproduction of lactic acid and the impaired mitochondrial uptake and utilization of lactate/pyruvate.

While reduced ATP availability results in enhanced activity of phosphofructokinase and increased lactate production, decreased cytosolic pH, a consequence of lactic acid overproduction, inhibits the activity of the enzyme. The inhibition of organic acid production by intracellular acid and the converse, increase in organic acid production observed when intracellular hydrogen ion is reduced, serves as a servomechanism to stabilize intracellular pH. Inhibition of phosphofructokinase activity by H^+ in lactic acidosis may be interpreted as evidence that protection of intracellular pH takes precedence over energy requirements during extreme anaerobiasis.

It should be clear from this discourse that lactate is produced in all tissues. In some tissues (skeletal muscle, skin, brain, renal medulla, erythrocytes, leucocytes, and platelets) glycolysis is the predominant source of energy and as a consequence, lactate is produced, that is, the venous concentration of lactate exceeds the arterial concentration. The liver, renal cortex, and heart utilize lactate for gluconeogenesis, the synthesis of lipids, or for the generation of energy by further oxidation to CO_2 and water. These tissues remove lactate from arterial blood. The equilibrium between production of lactate and lactate uptake results in a resting plasma lactate concentration of about 1 mmol/L. The extraction and utilization of lactate by the liver and renal cortex increase markedly when plasma lactate concentration is increased by infusion. During prolonged exercise lactate production by muscle increases markedly but plasma lactate increases only minimally, evidence of the large capacity of the liver and renal cortex for lactate uptake. Lactate is filtered at the glomerulus and actively reabsorbed. The renal threshold for lactate is 5 to 6 mEq/L. Only a small fraction of filtered lactate is excreted in the urine.

The common factor in the many clinical conditions which give rise to lactic acidosis is a defect in mitochondrial energy metabolism. Typically lactic acidosis is associated with decreased oxygen delivery to tissues as a consequence of decreased tissue perfusion, decreased cardiac output or hypotension, or reduced oxygen content of blood (hypoxia or profound anemia.) Less commonly, mitochondrial energy metabolism is impaired by drugs (such as ethanol, methanol, or biguanides such as phenformin), toxins (such as cyanide or nitroprusside), or by severe hepatic dysfunction. Impaired mitochondrial oxidation results in both the *overproduction of lactic acid* and the *impaired utilization* of lactate.

The overproduction of lactic acid within the cytosol of tissues in which mitochondrial oxidation is impaired results in the generation of protons and leads to intracellular acidosis. Lactic acid, with a $pK = 3.8$, is virtually completely ionized to H^+ and lactate$^-$ at cytosolic pH. Both the lactate and the protons exit the cell and appear in the extracellular fluid. In the extracellular fluid, protons combine with bicarbonate and nonbicarbonate buffers; plasma bicarbonate concentration declines. Lactate ions added to the extracellular fluid contribute to the anion gap. The magnitude of these changes, that is, the decrement in plasma bicarbonate concentration ($\triangle HCO_3^-$) and the increment in "unmeasured anions" ($\triangle$ anion gap), are often closely matched. In other words, the ratio, $\triangle HCO_3^-/\triangle$ anion gap, sometimes referred to as the $\triangle/\triangle$, approximates a value of 1 in untreated lactic acidosis, suggesting the addition of equimolar amounts of lactate and protons to the extracellular fluid. This has been a puzzling observation. Neither lactate nor hydrogen ion diffuse freely out of cells and the exit of these ions, in equimolar quantities, by diffusion seems unlikely. Alternatively, it might be that lactic acid diffuses out of cells and dissociates to yield H^+ and lactate. However, since the pK of lactic acid is 3.8, the ratio of lactic acid to lactate at intracellular pH is less than 1:1000. Diffusion of only the nonionized lactic acid would require that more than 99.9 percent of the lactic acid be titrated by intracellular buffers. It seems more likely that, in response to acute overproduction, protons and lactate ions are both actively transported out of cells. In amphibian and mammalian renal proximal tubular cells, the extrusion of protons and monocarboxylates across the plasma membrane are linked by a basolateral cotransporter. H^+-lactate cotransporters (symporters) have been described in a wide variety of cells. These utilize the hydrogen ion gradient to move a proton and lactate in the same direction. Under most circumstances, the $[H^+]$ gradient is *inwardly directed* and the cotransport process mediates lactate *uptake*. In tissues undergoing lactic acid overproduction, the H^+-lactate cotransporter might transport H^+ and lactate out of the cell in response to an increase in intracellular hydrogen ion concentration. Cotransport of H^+ and lactate into the extracellular fluid would provide a reasonable alternative explanation for the near equimolar addition of excess protons and lactate ions to the extracellular fluid in lactic acidosis.

Treatment in lactic acidosis should be focused on correcting the underlying disorder which gives rise to lactic acid overproduction, that is, correcting shock, hypoxia, or sepsis. The administration of sodium bicarbonate, to correct metabolic acidosis, often requires the infusion of extremely large quantities of bicarbonate with the risk of volume expansion, hypernatremia, and hyperosmolality. As noted above, increased intracellular hydrogen ion concentration inhibits the glycolytic cycle and slows the rate of lactic acid production. Correcting metabolic acidosis by bicarbonate administration might have the paradoxic effect of increasing glycolysis and lactic acid production. Finally, as will be described in a later chapter (p. 116), bicarbonate administration often leads to severe "rebound alkalosis" during the recovery phase of lactic acidosis. Lactic acidosis is often severe with extracellular pH values at 7.0 or lower. The magnitude of the decrease in intracellular pH is not known. The derangement in cellular functions and the hemodynamic consequences of such marked metabolic acidosis usually dictate the intravenous administration of sodium bicarbonate. The rate of acid generation is often 100 to 300 mmol/h; bicarbonate administration at comparable rates soon leads to extracellular fluid volume expansion and hypernatremia, which may necessitate dialysis.

Since it appears that failure to metabolize pyruvate is the underlying metabolic defect responsible for lactate overproduction, efforts to stimulate pyruvate utilization have been sought. The administration of the drug, dichloracetate, which enhances the activity of pyruvate dehydrogenase, has been tried with limited success.

Ketoacid Overproduction

The other major form of "overproduction metabolic acidosis" is keto-acidosis. Most commonly this occurs in insulin-deficient diabetes mellitus but it can be seen during fasting in alcoholics and in patients with hereditary deficiency of enzymes required for glucose synthesis (glucose-6-phosphatase or fructose-1,6-biphosphatase).

When glucose metabolism is impaired by insulin deficiency, several hormones are secreted in excess. Plasma concentrations of glucagon, cortisol, growth hormone, and epinephrine are all elevated to a variable degree in insulin-deficient states. "Hormone-sensitive" lipase, normally inhibited by relatively low concentrations of insulin, is stimulated by glucagon, growth hormone, cortisol, and epinephrine. These "lipokinetic" hormones serve to release free fatty acids from their storage form, tri-glyceride, in adipose tissue to provide an alternative substrate for energy production. Free fatty acids are readily taken up by the liver, muscle, and other tissues. In diabetic ketoacidosis, the production of free fatty acids exceeds the uptake and utilization by muscle and other nonhepatic tissues. The hepatic uptake of free fatty acids is markedly increased. When insulin is available, fatty acids are esterified in the hepatic cytosol with glycerol to regenerate triglycerides. When insulin is deficient, the uptake of free fatty acids is followed by enzymatic conversion to fatty acyl–CoA derivatives in the hepatic cytosol. These long-chain fatty acid derivatives are actively transported across the mitochondrial membrane by an enzyme embedded in the mitochrondrial membrane. This enzyme, fatty acyl carnitine transferase, catalyzes the formation of an ester be-tween the fatty acyl–CoA and carnitine. This uncharged molecule diffuses across the mitochrondrial membrane and is reconverted to fatty acyl–CoA on the matrix side of the membrane. The enzyme functions much in the manner of a membrane transport protein. The activity of carnitine transferase is regulated by both glucagon and insulin. Increased glucagon concentration and decreased insulin concentration in plasma increase the activity of carnitine transferase and thereby facilitate mitochondrial uptake of acyl–CoA derivatives. Within the mitochondrion, acyl-CoA oxidation through the Krebs cycle is limited by low concentrations of oxaloacetate; fatty acyl–CoA undergoes β-oxidation to acetyl-CoA.

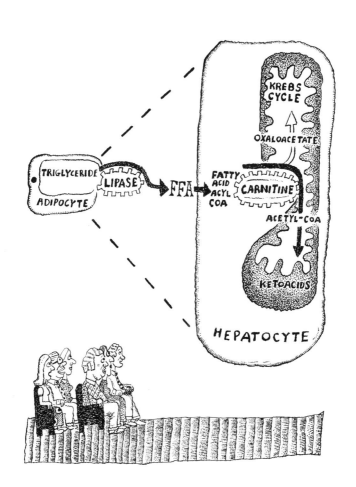

Acetyl-CoA molecules condense to form beta-hydroxybutyric and acetoacetic acid. These are usually referred to as ketoacids, but in fact only acetoacetic acid is a true *keto*acid; the keto group is reduced in beta-hydroxybutyric acid. The ratio of these fatty acids is determined by the mitochondrial $NADH/NAD^+$ ratio. A lower redox potential favors the production of beta-hydroxybutyric acid.

$$CH_3-\overset{\overset{\displaystyle O}{\|}}{C}-CH_2-\overset{\overset{\displaystyle O}{\|}}{C}-OH + H^+ \underset{\longrightarrow}{\overset{NADH}{\rightleftharpoons}} CH_3-\overset{\overset{\displaystyle OH}{|}}{C}-CH_2-\overset{\overset{\displaystyle O}{\|}}{C}-OH$$

(acetoacetic acid) NAD^+ (beta-hydroxybutyric acid)

In severe ketoacidosis, ketoacid production may be as high as 1000 to 2000 mmol/day. There is evidence of a feedback control of ketoacid production; acidemia inhibits and alkalemia accelerates ketoacid overproduction.

The pK of both acids is quite low (acetoacetic acid = 3.6, beta-hydroxybutyric acid = 4.4), and both are therefore almost completely ionized at intracellular or plasma pH. The acid load presented by ketoacid overproduction, like that seen in lactic acidosis, titrates cellular and extracellular (bicarbonate) buffers. In untreated diabetic ketoacidosis, the increase in anion gap, an indirect measure of the plasma concentrations of acetoacetate and beta-hydroxybutyrate, closely approximates the decrement in plasma bicarbonate concentration, that is, ketoacidosis is characterized by an increased anion gap. As noted for lactic acidosis, the nearly one-to-one relationship between fall in bicarbonate concentration and increase in anion gap ($\triangle/\triangle = 1$) suggests that protons and ketoacid anions generated by cellular metabolism are transported into the extracellular fluid by a common cotransport system, possibly a H^+-monocarboxylate cotransporter.

Acetoacetic acid and beta-hydroxybutyric acid are freely filtered at the glomerulus. Proximal tubular reabsorption is limited and may further decrease in response to systemic acidemia; ketoacids are excreted in the urine when the plasma concentration exceeds about 2 mmol/L. In contrast to lactate, acetoacetate and beta-hydroxybutyrate excretion is often considerable, as high as 100 to 400 mmol/24 h. At the pH of plasma and glomerular filtrate the ketoacids are almost completely ionized to acetoacetate and beta-hydroxybutyrate and serve as buffers for protons secreted in the collecting tubule. With pK values of 3.6 and 4.4, at the minimal urinary pH, the ratio base/acid approximates 1, that is, approximately one proton can be excreted for every two molecules of acetoacetate or beta-hydroxybutyrate excreted. When the urine is maximally acid, distal hydrogen ion excretion may increase by 50 to 200 mmol/day as a consequence of the buffer provided by ketoacid anion excretion. Ketoacid anion excretion obligates the excretion of other cations, mainly sodium and potassium, and often results in clinically significant extracellular volume depletion and potassium loss.

Peripheral tissues utilize acetoacetate and beta-hydroxybutyrate as metabolic substrates; this capacity is enhanced when insulin is administered. The oxidative metabolism of acetoacetate and beta-hydroxybutyrate consumes hydrogen ion, mole for mole, and recovery from ketoacidosis (with insulin treatment) is characterized by equimolar ketoacid consumption and bicarbonate regeneration. Were it not for the urinary loss of ketoacid anions, tissue oxidation of ketoacid acids would result in complete correction of metabolic acidosis with proportionate reductions in the anion gap and the bicarbonate deficit. The substantial urinary loss of acetoacetate and beta-hydroxybutyrate (base equivalents) in ketoacidosis mimics the loss of bicarbonate, with sodium and potassium, in proximal RTA. This appears to explain the observation that during the recovery phase following insulin administration, diabetic keto-acidosis may be marked by hyperchloremia and a normal anion gap. This hyperchloremic metabolic acidosis is transient and corrected by renal tubular bicarbonate generation. Except when metabolic acidosis is unusually severe, the treatment of diabetic ketoacidosis consists of insulin administration and replacement of sodium, potassium, and fluid losses; bicarbonate administration is not often required.

Ketoacidosis associated with starvation, attributed to the combination of low insulin levels and elevated levels of counterregulatory (lipokinetic) hormones, is typically mild despite production of large quantities of ketoacid. It seems likely that the slow onset of starvation ketosis is associated with more efficient compensatory increase in renal acid excretion, which offsets the overproduction of acid.

Alcoholic ketoacidosis is usually seen in the setting of decreased caloric intake following an alcoholic binge. Ketoacid overproduction is stimulated by low insulin levels and increased circulating levels of cortisol, glucagon, and growth hormone. The unique feature of alcoholic ketoacidosis is the preponderant overproduction of beta-hydroxybutyric acid as compared with acetoacetic acid. This finding is explained by the increased redox potential ($NADH/NAD^+$) within the hepatic cytosol. Ethanol metabolism reduces NAD^+ to NADH, and ethanol-induced mitochondrial injury may hinder regeneration of oxidized NAD^+.

The clinical tests for "acetone," which are usually strongly positive in diabetic ketoacidosis and starvation ketosis, may be negative or equivocal in alcoholic ketoacidosis as these reagents react with the carbonyl or ketone moiety of acetoacetate which is replaced by a hydroxyl group in beta-hydroxybutyric acid. Since beta-hydroxybutyric acid is not in fact a "ketoacid," this disorder in alcoholics might more correctly be termed "alcoholic beta-hydroxybutyric acidosis."

Metabolic acidosis can result from the accidental or suicidal ingestion of a variety of substances which are metabolized to weak or strong acids. In each instance, the generation of an acid provides a proton; whether the anion gap is increased or not is dependent on the renal excretion of the associated anion. Methanol causes acidosis with an *increased anion gap* made up of formic acid. Metabolic acidosis in ethylene glycol (antifreeze) ingestion is due to accumulation of the metabolic products glycolic acid, glyoxylic acid, and oxalic acid; the anion gap is increased by these anions. The ingestion of hydrochloric acid or ammonium chloride leads to hyperchloremic metabolic acidosis since they do not increase the concentration of unmeasured ions. Metabolic acidosis associated with the inhalation of toluene ("glue sniffing") is caused by the production of hippuric acid. This anion is readily excreted by the kidney and hippurate does not contribute to the anion gap; metabolic acidosis associated with "glue sniffing" is a *normal anion gap acidosis*. Similarly, metabolic acidosis may result from the ingestion of large quantities of methionine, which is metabolized to sulfuric acid. Since sulfate is secreted by the renal tubule, this anion does not accumulate and a normal anion gap metabolic acidosis results.

Metabolic Acidosis Secondary to Extrarenal Base Loss

Metabolic acidosis also results from the loss of bicarbonate or base equivalents from the gastrointestinal tract. Base equivalents are organic anions (such as lactate, acetate, citrate) which can be absorbed from the gastrointestinal tract and metabolized to bicarbonate.

In addition to the secretion of more than 250 mmol of bicarbonate in pancreatic, biliary and duodenal secretions, about 60 mmol of "base equivalent" organic anions are present as dietary components or are generated by digestive processes. From the viewpoint of acid–base balance, the net result of a great deal of interesting organ and cellular ion transport in the gastrointestinal tract is the absorption of 30 to 60 mmol of dietary "base equivalent" and the loss of 15 to 20 mmol of bicarbonate in stool.

While the loss of gastric fluid represents a loss of hydrogen ion and results in *metabolic alkalosis*, external drainage of biliary, pancreatic, or small intestinal fluids, all of which contain bicarbonate in concentrations higher than that of plasma, results in *metabolic acidosis*. Diarrhea, whether due to secretion of fluid and electrolyte in the small bowel (secretory diarrhea), or impaired fluid and electrolyte reabsorption in the colon, causes loss of a variable quantity of bicarbonate. If bicarbonate in the colon is titrated by organic acids generated by intestinal flora, diarrheal fluid may be acid and yet contain organic anions representing bicarbonate or "base equivalents."

The gastrointestinal loss of bicarbonate or "base equivalents" results in metabolic acidosis. The loss of bicarbonate via the gastrointestinal tract is associated with the loss of anions, predominantly sodium and potassium. Hydrogen ion secretion in the distal nephron and renal ammoniagenesis increase. Tubular sodium reabsorption, with chloride to maintain extracellular fluid volume, leads, as in RTA, to hyperchloremia.

It is not always easy to distinguish between hyperchloremic metabolic acidosis in proximal or some forms of distal RTA and hyperchloremic acidosis resulting from gastrointestinal bicarbonate loss. At times the severity of diarrheal losses is difficult to assess. In both clinical conditions the urine pH may be acid. Calculation of the *urine anion gap* can be very helpful in this situation. Under normal conditions, the major urinary anions are chloride and, in alkaline or neutral urine, bicarbonate; the contribution of phosphate and sulfate is small and closely related to the composition of the diet. The predominant urinary cations are sodium and potassium. Ammonium (NH_4^+) represents another urinary cation, but it is not measured in most clinical laboratories. Under normal acid base conditions, urinary ammonium excretion is about 50 mmol/day so that the concentration of this cation is approximately 30 to 50 mmol/L. In chronic metabolic acidosis, as might be seen with chronic diarrhea, ammonia production is greatly increased and urinary ammonium excretion may reach 300 mmol/day. Calculation of the urinary anion gap, the sum of the measured concentrations of sodium and potassium minus the urinary chloride concentration (bicarbonate concentration is negligible in urine when pH is <6.5), yields a large negative quantity, an indirect measure of urinary ammonium concentration. In contrast, in renal tubular acidosis, ammonium excretion is limited by impaired urinary acidification and this large "negative urinary anion gap" is not observed.

The urinary anion gap is increased, that is, the sum of urinary sodium and potassium exceeds the chloride concentration, in forms of metabolic acidosis due to the overproduction of acetoacetic, beta-hydroxybutyric, sulfuric, or hippuric acid whose (unmeasured) anions are excreted by the kidney.

In some forms of chronic metabolic acidosis, the urinary concentrations of both unmeasured cation (ammonium) and unmeasured anion (organic anion) are increased. This can be suspected when the measured urinary *osmolality* is significantly greater than the osmolality estimated from the sum of the measured millimolar concentrations of sodium, potassium, chloride, bicarbonate, glucose, and urea.

12

Metabolic Alkalosis:
With or Without Chloride

Metabolic alkalosis, a primary decrease in cellular and extracellular hydrogen ion concentration, is characterized by increased plasma concentration of bicarbonate. Metabolic alkalosis is generated by either the inappropriate loss of hydrogen ion or the excessive intake of bicarbonate or anions such as lactate, acetate, or citrate which are metabolized to yield bicarbonate. The prodigious ability of the kidney to excrete bicarbonate, however, requires that additional physiologic derangements must be present for metabolic alkalosis to be maintained.

The administration of sodium bicarbonate, by mouth or by infusion, normally produces only a small and transient increase in plasma bicarbonate concentration. Even the administration of rather massive quantities of sodium bicarbonate fails to induce significant elevation of plasma bicarbonate concentration. During bicarbonate loading, small increments in plasma bicarbonate are associated with extracellular fluid volume expansion and mild alkalemia. Renal bicarbonate excretion increases, primarily as a consequence of decreased *proximal* tubular hydrogen ion secretion and delivery of a greater fraction of the increased filtered load of bicarbonate to the distal nephron.

Inhibition of collecting tubule acid secretion can contribute little to the excretion of bicarbonate since collecting duct hydrogen ion secretion (mediated by H^+-ATPAse) and renal ammoniagenesis together account for only about 50 mmol of acid secreted (or bicarbonate generated) daily. How much cortical collecting duct bicarbonate secretion by β-intercalated cells adds to overall renal bicarbonate excretion is not known.

Early studies, utilizing bicarbonate infusion and whole kidney clearance techniques, suggested that proximal bicarbonate reabsorption might be limited by a maximum transport rate. While direct measurements in proximal tubules perfused with bicarbonate confirm the presence of a limiting rate of bicarbonate reabsorption, the renal threshold for bicarbonate reabsorption is more likely a consequence of extracellular fluid volume expansion which accompanies the infusion of large quantities of sodium bicarbonate. Plasma and extracellular fluid volume expansion result in both an increase in filtration rate and inhibition of bicarbonate reabsorption. The increased filtration of bicarbonate and the decreased tubular reabsorption (mediated by Na^+-H^+ exchange) result in bicarbonate excretion with very little increase in plasma bicarbonate concentration.

Chloride-Responsive Metabolic Alkalosis

Many of the clinical circumstances in which metabolic alkalosis develops and is maintained are characterized by reduced plasma volume or extracellular fluid volume, a reduction in glomerular filtration rate (hence a decrease in the filtered load of bicarbonate), and increased proximal tubular Na^+-H^+ exchange. The maintenance phase of metabolic alkalosis, whether generated by hydrogen ion loss or by base gain, requires an increase in proximal bicarbonate reabsorption. The reabsorption of bicarbonate in the proximal tubule is governed by the relative quantities of bicarbonate filtered and protons secreted by the proximal tubule Na^+-H^+ antiporter. Angiotensin II is a potent stimulus for proximal Na^+-H^+ antiporter activity. Reduced extracellular fluid volume stimulates the renin-angiotensin system and the angiotensin II generated exerts an important effect on proximal tubule bicarbonate reabsorption. Angiotensin II binding to specific receptors on the luminal and basolateral surfaces of the proximal tubular cell activates a G protein which inhibits adenylate cyclase and leads to a fall in the concentration of cyclic AMP (see pp. 37–38). Since cyclic AMP is an inhibitor of the proximal tubular sodium–hydrogen antiporter, angiotensin II "releases" this inhibition and stimulates Na^+-H^+ antiporter activity and bicarbonate "reabsorption."

Additional factors contribute to the maintenance of increased plasma bicarbonate concentration in metabolic alkalosis. Elevation of pCO_2, a part of the physiologic compensatory response in metabolic alkalosis, stimulates Na^+-H^+ antiporter activity. Further, the increased concentration of bicarbonate in proximal tubule fluid facilitates Na^+-H^+ exchange by providing Na^+ for exchange and by buffering the secreted protons.

A unifying feature of many clinical conditions in which metabolic alkalosis is associated with a decreased filtered load of bicarbonate and increased proximal Na^+-H^+ exchange is *chloride deficiency*. The loss of chloride may come about as a result of gastric fluid losses, diuretic administration, increased renal excretion, or, rarely, from loss in diarrheal fluid. The decrease in chloride from the extracellular fluid leads to a reduction in extracellular fluid volume and decreased glomerular filtration rate; the renin-angiotensin system is stimulated. Urinary chloride excretion is usually near zero in these states. The measurement of urinary chloride concentration is a valuable tool in determining whether metabolic alkalosis will respond to chloride replacement. The administration of chloride, regardless of the associated cation, is often sufficient to correct the acid–base abnormality in these "*chloride-responsive*" forms of metabolic alkalosis. The correction is, in large part, attributable to correction of the extracellular fluid volume deficit and suppression of renal renin release. Additionally, the delivery of chloride to distal nephron segments may facilitate bicarbonate secretion via the chloride-bicarbonate exchanger on the apical border of β-intercalated cells in the cortical collecting tubule.

"Chloride-responsive" metabolic alkalosis results when chloride deficiency, extracellular fluid depletion, and activation of the renin-angiotensin system impair the kidney's ability to respond to either the administration of base (bicarbonate or organic anion metabolized to bicarbonate) or the loss of hydrogen ion. Perhaps the most common example of metabolic alkalosis associated with base administration is seen in patients receiving lactate-Ringer's solution as parenteral fluid replacement following surgery or extensive trauma. In this setting, volume depletion with chloride depletion, often subtle in its hemodynamic manifestations, impairs renal bicarbonate excretion and permits the accumulation of bicarbonate derived from the oxidative metabolism of lactate resulting in metabolic alkalosis.

"Rebound" metabolic alkalosis may be sudden in onset and severe in patients with lactic acidosis or diabetic ketoacidosis, treated with sodium bicarbonate. During the recovery from lactic acidosis or ketoacidosis organic anions are metabolized to bicarbonate; the sum of generated bicarbonate and bicarbonate infused to correct the initial metabolic acidosis often yields a plasma bicarbonate concentration above 40 mmol/L and marked alkalemia. Extracellular fluid volume and chloride depletion, common findings in lactic acidosis and diabetic ketoacidosis, impair the ability of the kidney to excrete the bicarbonate load.

More commonly, chloride deficiency and the consequent derangements which facilitate bicarbonate reabsorption serve to maintain metabolic alkalosis which is generated by the renal or extrarenal loss of hydrogen ion. The best studied example of metabolic alkalosis due to loss of hydrogen ion is that associated with loss of gastric fluid, either by vomiting or gastric suction. Large quantities of hydrogen ion and chloride, often in excess of 300 mmol/day, can be lost via gastric drainage or vomiting. The immediate biochemical response to the loss of this quantity of hydrogen ion is an increase in plasma bicarbonate concentration attributable to a shift in the equilibrium,

$$H_2CO_3 \rightleftharpoons H^+ + HCO_3^-$$

When $[H^+]$ falls, the dissociation of carbonic acid yields bicarbonate and protons. The extracellular fluid hydrogen ion concentration increases toward normal while the bicarbonate concentration becomes elevated. The plasma pH is usually somewhat alkaline. Renal acid excretion decreases; modest bicarbonaturia (and sodium loss) ensues but cannot correct the acute metabolic alkalosis as long as gastric fluid drainage continues.

More importantly, unless the chloride deficit created by gastric fluid loss is corrected by resumption of dietary intake or intravenous replacement, metabolic alkalosis is persistent even when gastric fluid drainage or vomiting cease. During this "maintenance phase" of metabolic alkalosis, the urine is acid and renal net acid excretion (representing collecting tubule acidification and renal ammoniagenesis) match the daily metabolic acid production. The proximal and distal convoluted tubules secrete the increased quantity of hydrogen ion, via Na^+-H^+ exchange, required to "reabsorb" the increased load of filtered bicarbonate. Continued renal acid excretion despite metabolic alkalosis presents a paradox. Why doesn't the kidney ("in its wisdom") either decrease proximal bicarbonate reabsorption or decrease collecting tubule acid secretion? Why does acid secretion persist despite systemic alkalosis? Consideration of the factors responsible for continued acid secretion during the "maintenance phase" of metabolic alkalosis make this form of "gastric alkalosis" very instructive.

Several factors probably serve to maintain *proximal* tubular hydrogen ion secretion and bicarbonate reabsorption in the face of systemic alkalosis. Extracellular fluid volume contraction, a consequence of the initial gastric chloride loss and the subsequent urinary excretion of sodium with bicarbonate, contributes to excessive proximal bicarbonate reabsorption; this is probably mediated by increased levels of angiotensin II. The respiratory compensation in metabolic alkalosis, hypoventilation and consequent increased $PaCO_2$, may also play a role. As discussed earlier, elevated levels of CO_2 in plasma stimulate the proximal tubule Na^+-H^+ antiporter. This represents an instance in which "proximal tubular hydrogen ion secretion mediated by the Na^+-H^+ antiporter appears more intimately related to the maintenance of sodium balance than to acid–base homeostasis" (p. 84). Significant bicarbonate rejection by the proximal tubule would result in urinary losses of sodium and potassium as cations associated with urinary bicarbonate.

Urinary acidification, in the face of systemic alkalosis, is attributable to continued activity of the proton-translocating ATPase (H^+-ATPase) in the *collecting* tubule. H^+ secretion in both the cortical and medullary collecting tubules is stimulated by aldosterone which is secreted in excess in response to extracellular volume depletion and increased activity of the renin-angiotensin system. Chloride depletion plays an important role in promoting H^+ secretion in the cortical collecting tubule. In this nephron segment, sodium reabsorption generates a lumen-negative potential which is dissipated by chloride reabsorption. Sodium reabsorption (stimulated by aldosterone) in the absence of chloride generates a lumen-negative potential and thereby facilitates proton secretion.

Although decreased glomerular filtration, increased angiotensin II and aldosterone concentrations, and increased $PaCO_2$ all serve to increase bicarbonate reabsorption and acid secretion, the most important factor in maintaining metabolic alkalosis following gastric fluid loss is the chloride deficit incurred with the loss of gastric fluid. The urine is usually chloride-free in this maintenance phase.

Treatment by repletion of the chloride deficit with any chloride salt, generally sodium or potassium chloride are given, leads to prompt correction of "gastric alkalosis"—hence this is classified as a "chloride-responsive" form of metabolic alkalosis. How does chloride, which is not an acid, correct metabolic alkalosis? Chloride has its effects at several levels. First, chloride administration permits correction of the extracellular fluid volume deficit which results from gastric fluid loss. Next, chloride plays a role in the regulation of the renin-angiotensin-aldosterone system. Correction of the chloride deficit suppresses the overproduction of renin, angiotensin II, and aldosterone which are seen with gastric fluid loss. Finally, when the chloride deficit is repaired, chloride is delivered to the collecting tubule segments. In the cortical collecting tubule, chloride reabsorption reduces the lumen negativity which follows sodium reabsorption; the electrochemical gradient favoring H^+ secretion is decreased. In the medullary collecting duct, as luminal chloride concentration rises, chloride conductance, which permits movement of chloride from cell to lumen and facilitates proton secretion in this segment, is reduced. The presence of chloride in the collecting tubule fluid may permit bicarbonate secretion by intercalated cells with apical membrane Cl^-/bicarbonate exchangers (β-intercalated cells). The net effect of chloride administration is the prompt correction of metabolic alkalosis with the renal excretion of bicarbonate.

"Chloride-responsive" metabolic alkalosis is also frequently observed following diuretic administration. Here we must consider the factors which generate the alkalosis and those factors which are responsible for its maintenance. Most diuretics act at either the ascending loop of Henle (e.g., furosemide) or the distal convoluted tubule (e.g., thiazides). Inhibition of sodium and chloride reabsorption does not directly affect acid–base balance but leads to increased activity of the renin-angiotensin system and increased aldosterone secretion. Inhibition of sodium reabsorption at the loop of Henle or distal convoluted tubule results in the presentation of an increased quantity of sodium to the cortical collecting tubule where sodium reabsorption, stimulated by aldosterone, generates an electrochemical driving force for proton secretion. Increased aldosterone binding to receptors on cells in medullary collecting duct segments stimulates sodium-independent proton secretion. Excessive distal nephron acid secretion results in metabolic alkalosis. Proximal bicarbonate reabsorption is stimulated by the combined effects of reduced glomerular filtration (associated with diuretic administration and the underlying disorder which called for diuretic therapy) and by increased plasma angiotensin II concentration.

The factors responsible for excessive distal hydrogen ion secretion in metabolic alkalosis, that is, increased distal sodium delivery and aldosterone excess, also lead to increased potassium secretion and to potassium depletion. The frequent association of hypokalemia with metabolic alkalosis following diuretic administration has suggested a role for potassium depletion in the maintenance of the alkalosis. It has been suggested that loss of intracellular potassium might result in a shift of hydrogen ions into cells with resultant fall in intracellular pH. Potassium depletion in renal tubular cells might result in inappropriate, that is, excessive, hydrogen ion secretion and thereby play a role in maintaining metabolic alkalosis. Further, potassium depletion stimulates proximal tubular hypertrophy, renal glutaminase activity, and renal ammoniagenesis. Potassium depletion has been reported to stimulate the H^+-K^+ ATPase in collecting tubule cells. This transporter might provide an additional source of secreted protons to maintain metabolic alkalosis in potassium depletion. Since selective potassium depletion, induced either by diet or, experimentally, by hemodialysis, does not result in alkalosis, it seems likely hypokalemia exerts a permissive rather than a primary role in diuretic-induced metabolic alkalosis.

Diuretic-induced metabolic alkalosis, like metabolic alkalosis secondary to gastric acid loss, is "chloride responsive." Usually chloride is given in the form of potassium chloride to avoid administration of sodium; correction of alkalosis is attributed (probably incorrectly) to potassium rather than chloride.

Chloride loss, with resultant metabolic alkalosis, is also seen in Bartter's syndrome, an uncommon disorder characterized by renal sodium, potassium and chloride wasting which appears to be due to a decreased activity of the $Na^+-K^+-2Cl^-$ cotransporter in the thick ascending limb of Henle. Metabolic alkalosis, which may be severe, is attributable to several factors. Marked elevation of plasma renin activity, angiotensin II concentration, and aldosterone secretion are typical in Bartter's syndrome. Angiotensin II stimulates increased proximal tubular bicarbonate reabsorption and aldosterone stimulates collecting duct sodium reabsorption and hydrogen ion secretion. However, these factors cannot fully explain the persistent metabolic alkalosis. Neither inhibition of renin secretion nor blocking the actions of aldosterone with spironolactone, a competitive antagonist of aldosterone, corrects the metabolic alkalosis and potassium wasting. It seems likely that chloride deficit, due to the underlying defect in loop chloride transport, plays a major role in this form of alkalosis.

Chloride-Resistant Metabolic Alkalosis

Not all forms of metabolic alkalosis can be attributed to volume contraction, reduced GFR, increased angiotensin II concentration, or chloride depletion. Patients with excess production of adrenocortical hormones, either aldosterone, desoxycorticosterone or cortisol, exhibit chloride-resistant metabolic alkalosis. Such forms of metabolic alkalosis are not corrected by administration of sodium chloride. In these disorders, extracellular fluid volume is often *increased,* glomerular filtration rate may be *normal,* plasma renin activity and angiotensin II concentration are *reduced,* and there is no chloride deficit. The serum concentration of chloride is decreased (and the concentration of bicarbonate increased) equally in "chloride-responsive" and "chloride-resistant" metabolic alkalosis. Although the extracellular fluid chloride *concentration* is similar, the total quantity of chloride in body fluids differs considerably in these two forms of metabolic alkalosis.

The intracellular concentration of chloride is low, generally about 25 mmol/L. Most of the body's chloride is in the extracellular fluid compartment. In "chloride-responsive" metabolic alkalosis the extracellular fluid volume is decreased while "chloride-resistant" metabolic alkalosis is characterized by extracellular fluid volume expansion. Total exchangeable or extracellular chloride is therefore decreased in chloride-responsive metabolic alkalosis and normal or increased in "chloride-resistant" metabolic alkalosis. The generation of chloride-resistant metabolic alkalosis can be attributed to the mineralocorticoid effects of aldosterone or other salt-retaining adrenocortical hormones (such as DOC), which promote sodium reabsorption in the collecting tubule and thereby create an electrochemical gradient which favors proton secretion. While adrenocortical hormone excess may explain excess bicarbonate generation by collecting tubule acid secretion, it is not clear how proximal tubule bicarbonate reabsorption is increased in the maintenance phase of this form of metabolic alkalosis. It is not known whether proximal Na^+-H^+ exchange is increased in mineralocorticoid-induced metabolic alkalosis. It is possible that chronic stimulation of the distal acidifying mechanism causes an adaptive increase in H^+-ATPase such that bicarbonate delivered to the distal tubule no longer "overwhelms" the distal hydrogen secretory capacity as it does during acute bicarbonate loading. Chronic potassium depletion, which is an important feature of mineralocorticoid excess, stimulates cell growth in proximal tubular segments and might increase proximal Na^+-H^+ antiporter activity. Similarly, potassium depletion promotes bicarbonate generation by stimulating renal ammoniagenesis. Increased collecting tubule H^+-K^+ ATPase activity, stimulated by potassium depletion, may contribute to renal acid secretion.

In this form of *chloride-resistant* metabolic alkalosis, potassium replacement may partially correct the alkalosis. In most instances, the treatment of chloride-resistant metabolic alkalosis requires either surgical removal of the adrenal tumor responsible for excess adrenocortical hormone production or, in the case of aldosteronism due to bilateral adrenal hyperplasia, the administration of an aldosterone antagonist such as spironolactone or a "potassium-sparing" transport inhibitor such as amiloride.

13

Respiratory Disorders of Acid–Base Balance: The Wind Section

Respiratory acidosis is a consequence of impaired pulmonary excretion of CO_2. While CO_2 production may be increased in hypermetabolic states (e.g., fever, hyperthyroidism, exercise) the excess CO_2 is eliminated by the lung without change in the partial pressure of CO_2 in plasma ($PaCO_2$). Since CO_2 is highly diffusible across the pulmonary capillary and alveolar membranes, the rate of CO_2 removal is directly proportional to the rate of alveolar ventilation. Decreased alveolar ventilation leads to an increase in $PaCO_2$, hypercapnea; for any change in the rate of alveolar ventilation, a new steady-state level of $PaCO_2$, at which the pulmonary excretion of CO_2 is equal to metabolic production of CO_2, is usually attained within 10 to 15 minutes. As a consequence of increased partial pressure of CO_2, the plasma concentration of H_2CO_3 increases. The dissociation of H_2CO_3 yields equimolar quantities of H^+ and HCO_3^-. Since, at pH 7.4, the plasma concentration of H^+ is only $40 \times 10^{-9}\,M$ while that of HCO_3^- is almost one million times greater — $25 \times 10^{-3}\,M$ — the dissociation of H_2CO_3 has the effect of increasing the hydrogen ion concentration of plasma but does not change plasma bicarbonate concentration.

CO_2 diffuses freely across cell membranes. Protons generated when $PaCO_2$ increases acutely are buffered almost entirely by intracellular buffers, predominantly the histidine groups of intracellular proteins and hemoglobin. Doubling $PaCO_2$ from the normal value of 40 mmHg to

123

80 mmHg increases the plasma concentration of H_2CO_3 from 1.2 mM/L to 2.4 mM/L. If no buffering occurred the pH of plasma would fall from 7.4 to 7.1

$$pH = pK + \log \frac{HCO_3^-}{H_2CO_3}$$

at $PaCO_2$ 40 mmHg,

$$7.4 = 6.1 + \log \frac{24}{1.2} = 6.1 + 1.3$$

at $PaCO_2$ 80 mmHg,

$$7.1 = 6.1 + \log \frac{24}{2.4} = 6.1 + 1.0$$

The dissociation of H_2CO_3 within cells and the intracellular buffering of H^+, however, generates bicarbonate which is transported by chloride-bicarbonate exchange or $Na^+/3HCO_3^-$ cotransport into the plasma. The net effect of buffering the protons generated when $PaCO_2$ increases acutely from 40 to 80 mmHg is an increase in plasma bicarbonate concentration of 3 to 5 mM/L. The extracellular fluid pH therefore decreases only to 7.2.

$$7.2 = 6.1 + \log \frac{29}{2.4} = 6.1 + 1.1$$

Chronic respiratory acidosis occurs when alveolar ventilation is reduced by impairment of central respiratory regulation, chest wall dysfunction (skeletal, muscular, or neurologic disorders) or impaired airway mechanics (bronchospasm or emphysema), or impaired alveolar gas exchange. In chronic respiratory acidosis, the *biochemical* buffering of protons generated from H_2CO_3 is greatly augmented by *physiologic* compensation. Renal acid excretion increases and bicarbonate is thereby generated, resulting in increased plasma bicarbonate concentration.

As plasma bicarbonate concentration increases, chloride excretion is increased.

Why does chloride excretion increase? If you consider a urinary buffer such as phosphate, it will be apparent that the buffering of secreted H^+ changes the charge of the phosphate ion.

$$HPO_4^{-2} + H^+ \rightarrow H_2PO_4^-$$

Since electroneutrality of the urine must be maintained, this necessitates either the retention of a cation, presumably Na^+, or the excretion of another anion such as Cl^-. In fact, both electrolyte changes take place. Failure to acidify the urine in RTA results in sodium loss. Renal acidification in chronic respiratory acidosis leads to chloride loss.

This physiologic compensation, the renal excretion of acid and increase in plasma bicarbonate concentration, is quite effective in maintaining plasma pH at near normal levels despite substantial elevation of $PaCO_2$. The increase in plasma bicarbonate concentration offsets, in great measure, the increase in H_2CO_3 concentration. For example, in chronic respiratory acidosis with $PaCO_2 = 80\,mmHg$, plasma bicarbonate might increase to $45\,mmol/L$.

$$pH = 6.1 + \log\frac{45}{2.4} = 6.1 + 1.27 = 7.37$$

Increased $PaCO_2$ plays an important role in the maintenance of elevated plasma bicarbonate concentration by stimulating $Na^+–H^+$ exchange in the proximal tubule.

Whether $PaCO_2$ increases suddenly or gradually, the reduction in alveolar ventilation responsible for respiratory acidosis produces a concomitant impairment in oxygen delivery into the blood perfusing pulmonary capillaries. Arterial oxygen saturation is always reduced when alveolar ventilation is decreased, unless the concentration of oxygen in inspired air is increased. Arterial hypoxemia is usually a more important feature of the clinical presentation than is the respiratory acidosis. Respiratory acidosis without arterial oxygen unsaturation occasionally occurs during general anesthesia when alveolar hypoventilation goes unrecognized while hypoxemia is prevented by ventilation with oxygen-enriched gas mixtures. In sporadic case reports, and in animal experiments in which respiratory acidosis without hypoxemia has been studied, it appears that even extreme degrees of respiratory acidosis are remarkably well tolerated. In animals subjected to severe acute respiratory acidosis (arterial pH 6.9–7.0), measurements of pH in myocardium and brain revealed decrements in intracellular pH which were quite modest (0.05–0.15 pH unit). Buffering alone would not suffice to neutralize the large proton load imposed by these extreme degrees of hypercapnea. The maintenance of near normal intracellular pH in the face of markedly increased $PaCO_2$ indicates that cells possess effective means of transporting protons out of or bicarbonate into the cytosol to defend cellular pH. These transport processes ultimately require energy derived from oxidative metabolism. The ability to defend intracellular pH in the face of marked elevation of $PaCO_2$, when arterial oxygenation is maintained, is probably attributable to the preservation of membrane proton transport.

The primary focus of treatment in respiratory acidosis is the correction of the underlying ventilatory disorder. When this can be accomplished without resorting to assisted ventilation, correction of the acid–base disturbance follows *pari passu*. Clinically important acid–base disturbances often arise during the treatment of patients with chronic "compensated" respiratory acidosis when assisted ventilation (respirator therapy) is employed to increase the rate of alveolar ventilation. $PaCO_2$ can be reduced rapidly during assisted ventilation. Initially, the fall in $PaCO_2$ results in a fall in $[H^+]$ and may result in mild alkalemia. The appropriate compensatory renal responses, that is, decreased proximal bicarbonate reabsorption and increased urinary excretion of bicarbonate, like the renal compensation which resulted in bicarbonate accumulation, is slow, often requiring 24 to 48 hours. In patients rendered chloride deficient by dietary chloride restriction and excessive chloride excretion during the development of compensated respiratory acidosis, reducing $PaCO_2$ does not lead to increased bicarbonate excretion. The fall in $PaCO_2$ without a commensurate decline in plasma bicarbonate concentration results in a form of metabolic alkalosis termed "posthypercapnic alkalosis." While elevated $PaCO_2$ plays a central role in the generation and maintenance of elevated plasma bicarbonate concentration in chronic respiratory acidosis, chloride deficiency and decreased chloride availability in the collecting tubule appear to be the major determinants in the development and maintenance of posthypercapnic alkalosis.

The role of chloride depletion in the development and maintenance of "posthypercapnic alkalosis" in patients with respiratory acidosis is remarkably similar to the role of chloride in the maintenance of chloride-responsive metabolic alkalosis. Chloride depletion plays an important role in maintaining an elevated plasma bicarbonate concentration in both these disorders. Chloride deficiency in chronic respiratory acidosis leads to elevated plasma bicarbonate concentration through many of the same mechanisms which account for bicarbonate retention in chronic metabolic alkalosis. Chloride deficiency is associated with decreased glomerular filtration of bicarbonate. Activation of the renin-angiotensin system may result in angiotensin II stimulation of proximal tubule bicarbonate reabsorption. Chloride deficiency probably enhances collecting tubule acidification and may blunt tubular bicarbonate secretion.

Similarly, elevated $PaCO_2$, whether the result of impaired gas exchange in chronic respiratory acidosis or the result of "compensatory" reduction in alveolar ventilation in metabolic alkalosis, facilitates the reabsorption of bicarbonate in the proximal tubule. "Posthypercapnic" alkalosis and primary metabolic alkalosis probably coexist in many seriously ill patients in whom moderate chloride deficiency results from reduced dietary chloride intake and diuretic administration. This represents a form of mixed acid–base disorder in which the common feature is impaired renal excretion of bicarbonate. The biochemical features which characterize this mixed alkalosis are alkaline arterial pH, elevated plasma bicarbonate concentration, and elevated $PaCO_2$.

Administration of chloride, whether as a sodium or potassium salt, results in prompt correction of the inappropriate secretion of hydrogen ion which characterizes this disorder. Bicarbonate concentration falls and alkalosis is corrected; chloride is avidly retained during this process. When posthypercapneic alkalosis is severe, more rapid correction can be achieved by the administration of a carbonic anhydrase inhibitor such as acetazolamide, which inhibits hydrogen ion secretion and results in bicarbonaturia. Alternatively, an acidifying agent such as dilute hydro-chloric acid, ammonium chloride, or arginine hydrochloride may be given to correct alkalemia.

Respiratory alkalosis, a primary decrease in $[H^+]$ in blood, caused by decreased $PaCO_2$, is always attributable to an increase in the rate of alveolar ventilation. The clinical conditions which give rise to alveolar hyperventilation reflect abnormalities of each of the mechanisms which are known to control ventilation. Ventilation is under the control of neurons in the cerebral cortex, the brainstem (medullary) respiratory center, and peripheral (spinal cord) neurons which respond to input arising from chemoreceptors in the carotid and aortic bodies and within the brainstem itself. The central (medullary) chemoreceptors respond to cerebral interstitial hydrogen ion concentration. The peripheral chemoreceptors are stimulated by reduced arterial oxygen concentra-tion; when pO_2 falls below 60 mmHg, ventilation is stimulated.

Alveolar hyperventilation is stimulated by impaired oxygen exchange and hypoxemia in some forms of lung disease. Alveolar ventilation increases when arterial pH decreases in metabolic acidosis; this is usually viewed as "respiratory compensation" rather than "respiratory alkalosis." The stimulus for hyperventilation in metabolic acidosis is an accumu-lation of H^+ in the interstitium of the brain. During recovery from metabolic acidosis or following correction by the administration of alkali (bicarbonate), delayed diffusion of bicarbonate across the blood-brain barrier may result in persistent hyperventilation. This results in a true respiratory alkalosis which persists until bicarbonate diffusion into the central nervous system reaches equilibrium and hyperventilation ceases.

Alveolar hyperventilation results when the central or peripheral chemoreceptors are stimulated by agents such as salicylates, nicotine, or xanthines. Alveolar hyperventilation is seen in a variety of central nervous system diseases, in hepatic failure, and in gram negative sepsis. In anxiety states, the cortical control of respiration is probably the major mechanism responsible for hyperventilation. Finally, as was noted earlier, alveolar hyperventilation is "a way of life" for residents of high altitudes.

The loss of CO_2 by hyperventilation results in a decrease in the concentration of dissolved CO_2 and its hydration product, H_2CO_3. The fall in $[H^+]$ is buffered almost totally by nonbicarbonate buffers and is therefore largely accomplished by intracellular buffers. A decrease in $PaCO_2$ results in a fall in intracellular H^+ concentration. The dissociation of intracellular buffers yields hydrogen ions:

$$H - Buff \rightarrow H^+ + Buff^-$$

It is assumed that some fraction of the protons so generated are actively transported into the extracellular fluid but the transport systems which are responsible have not been defined.

An additional defense against the fall in hydrogen ion concentration associated with hypocapnia is the cellular generation of lactic acid. Earlier, it was pointed out that the activity of phosphofructokinase (PFK), one of the rate-limiting enzymes in glycolysis, is pH-dependent. In alkalosis PFK activity and the synthesis of lactic acid increases. The magnitude of the increase in plasma lactate concentration is generally small (1–3 mmol/L), suggesting that the contribution of this metabolic process to the correction of the extracellular H^+ deficit resulting from hypocapnia is not great. However, since lactic acid generation is intracellular, the contribution of protons derived from this source to intracellular buffering might be considerable if lactate extrusion (via a H^+-lactate cotransporter) is also inhibited by intracellular alkalosis.

The long-term compensatory response to respiratory alkalosis is a reduction in plasma bicarbonate concentration. This is accomplished by decreased renal bicarbonate generation. Little bicarbonate appears in the urine. The reduction in renal bicarbonate generation is attributable to reduced proximal Na^+–H^+ exchange and to decreased renal ammoniagenesis. Reduced Na^+–H^+ antiporter activity is likely due to reduced $PaCO_2$. It is thought that renal ammoniagenesis is partially inhibited by alkalosis. The ability of the kidney to excrete bicarbonate allows near perfect compensation for hyperventilation in otherwise healthy individuals such as high altitude dwellers. When the kidney's ability to excrete bicarbonate is impaired, by reduced filtration of bicarbonate or by physiologic derangements leading to sustained H^+ secretion (chloride deficiency, aldosterone excess, or stimulation of the renin-angiotensin system), alveolar hyperventilation may lead to marked alkalemia. This is most commonly seen in patients requiring assisted ventilation in intensive care units. Alveolar hyperventilation may be induced in order to maintain adequate blood oxygenation. In this setting, mixed respiratory and metabolic alkalosis is not uncommon. In this mixed disorder the combination of reduced $PaCO_2$ and elevated plasma bicarbonate concentration may result in severe alkalemia. Treatment of respiratory alkalosis is directed predominantly toward correction of the underlying disorder which stimulates alveolar hyperventilation. When respiratory and metabolic alkalosis coexist, particular attention should be focused on maintaining extracellular fluid volume and chloride balance.

EPILOGUE

I have attempted to "derive" an understanding of acid–base physiology from an examination of membrane transport mechanisms. I recognize the hazards of this approach. Information in the areas of molecular and cellular mechanisms of electrolyte transport is accumulating at a great rate. Some of the concepts outlined here will likely prove to be incomplete, naive, and possibly erroneous. Painful as such realizations will be for me, I am convinced that this approach can lead to a rational and coherent understanding of this subject.

Appendix I

Causes of Metabolic Acidosis

Impaired Renal Acid Secretion (or bicarbonate generation)

Specific defect in hydrogen ion secretion
    Distal tubular (distal or type I RTA)
    Proximal tubular (proximal or type II RTA)
    Impaired renal ammoniagenesis (type IV RTA)
        Aldosterone deficient (hyporeninemic hypoaldosteronism)
        Aldosterone resistant (obstructive uropathy)

Global (nonspecific) renal impairment
    Chronic renal parenchymal disease*
    Acute tubular necrosis*
    Renal papillary necrosis*
    Renal cortical necrosis*

Endogenous Acid Loading (metabolic acid overproduction)

Lactic acidosis*
Diabetic ketoacidosis*
Starvation ketosis*

Exogenous Acid Loading (acid ingestion)

Methanol ingestion*
Ethylene glycol ingestion*
Hydrochloric acid ingestion
Ammonium chloride ingestion
Toluene inhalation ("glue sniffing")

*Anion gap usually increased

Methionine overdosage
Salicylate ingestion*
Paraldehyde ingestion*

Loss of Bicarbonate

Carbonic anhydrase inhibition (acetazolamide)
Diarrhea
Pancreatic or biliary drainage
Urinary diversion (ileal bladder or conduit)

*Anion gap usually increased

Appendix II

Causes of Metabolic Alkalosis

Chloride-Responsive Metabolic Alkalosis

Loss of gastric fluid (vomiting or drainage)
Diuretic therapy
Posthypercapneic alkalosis
Rebound alkalosis following correction of organic acidosis
Administration of organic anions (e.g., penicillin) whose renal excretion obligates proton secretion
Chloride-losing diarrhea
"Contraction alkalosis"

Chloride-Resistant Metabolic Alkalosis

Aldosterone excess
  Primary aldosteronism
    Adrenal adenoma
    Bilateral adrenocortical hyperplasia
  Hyperreninic hypertension
    Malignant hypertension
    Renal artery stenosis
    Renin secreting tumor
  Exogenous administration
    Fludrocortisone (Florinef)
    High dose prednisone or methylprednisolone
Adrenocortical hypersecretion
  Cushing's syndrome
  ACTH hypersecretion or ectopic ACTH production
  DOC or other mineralocorticoid excess

Bartter's syndrome

Liddle's syndrome ("pseudoaldosteronism")

Alkalosis Secondary to Base Administration

Ingestion of large quantities of sodium bicarbonate
Milk-alkali syndrome
"Nonabsorbable antacid" ingestion
Multiple transfusions (citrate administration)

Appendix III

Causes of Respiratory Acidosis (Alveolar Hypoventilation)

Decreased Respiratory Drive

Oversedation
Narcotics
Brain lesions affecting the medulla (tumors, vascular, infectious, traumatic)
Obesity (Pickwickian syndrome)
Primary (Ondine's curse)

Impaired Ventilation

Neuromuscular impairment of chest wall function
Diaphragmatic paralysis
Kyphoscoliosis
Fibrothorax
Airway obstruction
    Chronic obstructive airway disease (emphysema)
    Bronchoconstriction (asthma)

Impaired Alveolar Gas Exchange

Increased respiratory dead space
Physiologic or anatomic shunts

Mechanical

Ventilator hypoventilation
Increased CO_2 content of inspired air

Appendix IV

Causes of Respiratory Alkalosis (Alveolar Hyperventilation)

Increased Central Respiratory Drive

Anxiety
Cerbrovascular disease
Cheyne-Stokes respiration

Hypoxia

High altitude
Pulmonary disease
    Decreased arterial oxygen saturation (hypoxemia)
Decreased arterial oxygen content (severe anemia)
Decreased cerebral blood flow (hypotension)

Tissue Acidosis

Persistent hyperventilation following correction of metabolic acidosis

Pharmacologic Stimulation of Respiration

Salicylates
Nicotine
Xanthines
Progesterone (pregnancy)

Hepatic Failure

Gram-Negative Sepsis

Mechanical

Ventilator hyperventilation

BIBLIOGRAPHY

Texts

Arieff, A. I., and De Fronzo, R. A., eds., *Fluid, Electrolyte and Acid Base Disorders,* Churchill-Livingston Inc., New York, Edinburgh, London, Melbourne, 1985.
Very good sections on intracellular pH and metabolic consequence of altered cellular pH.

Carroll, H. J., and Oh, M. S., *Water, Electrolyte and Acid–Base Metabolism: Diagnosis and Management,* 2nd ed., J. B. Lippincott, Philadelphia, 1989.
Excellent sections on hyperkalemia and type IV RTA.

Cohen, J. J., and Kassirer, J. P., *Acid/Base,* Little, Brown and Company, Boston, 1982.
The style and format of this excellent text reflects the close relation its authors have with the subject matter and each other. A fine section on comparative physiology.

Harold, F. M., *The Vital Force. A Study of Bioenergetics,* W. H. Freeman and Co., New York, 1986.
A remarkably clear exposition of the mechanisms which link energy utilization to membrane transport. The chapter on carriers, channels, and pumps is invaluable for readers interested in membrane transport.

Hills, A. G., *Acid–Base Balance,* Williams and Williams, Baltimore, 1973.
Most valuable for the lucid description of the properties of acids and bases and the role of buffering in acid–base homeostasis.

Seldin, D. W., and Giebisch, G., eds., *The Regulation of Acid–Base Balance,* Raven Press, New York, 1989.
This multi-authored text includes valuable sections on intracellular buffering, segmental hydrogen ion transport in the kidney, the role of the gastrointestinal tract, and the newer concepts of renal ammonium excretion.

Smith, H. W., *From Fish to Philosopher,* Little, Brown and Company, Boston, 1953.

Zadunaisky, J. A., ed., *Chloride Transport in Biological Membranes,* Academic Press, New York, 1982.
A valuable collection of papers describing the mechanism of chloride secretion in a variety of epithelial tissues.

Journal Articles and Reviews

Ion Transport

Al-Awqati, Q., "Proton-Translocating ATPases," *Ann. Rev. Cell Biol.,* 2: 179–199, 1986.
Well-written clear explanation of the types of proton pumps and their regulation.

Aronson, P. S., "Mechanisms of Active H^+ Secretion in the Proximal Tubule," *Am. J. Physiol.,* 245: F647–F659, 1983.
An important review of the mechanism of action and role of the renal proximal tubule Na^+–H^+ exchanger.

Hill, B., "Ionic Channels: Molecular Pores of Excitable Membranes," *The Harvey Lectures,* Series 82: 47–69, 1988.
A careful and detailed description of the structure and function of ion channels.

Lodish, H. F., "Anion-Exchange and Glucose Transport Proteins: Structure, Function, and Distribution," *The Harvey Lectures,* Series 82: 19–46, 1988.
Very complete description of the structure and function of two important transport proteins; highly technical.

"Molecular Aspects of Epithelial Transporters," *Hospital Practice,* January 15–July 15, 1989.
Benos, D. J., "The Biology of Amiloride-Sensitive Sodium Channels."
Brown, A. M., and Birnbaumer, L., "Ion Channels and G Proteins."
Culpepper, R. M., "Na^+–K^+–$2Cl^-$ Cotransport in the Thick Ascending Limb of Henle."
Dubinsky, W. P., Jr., "The Physiology of Epithelial Chloride Channels."
Gluck, S. L., "Cellular and Molecular Aspects of Renal H^+ Transport."
Silverman, M., "Molecular Biology of the Na^+–D-Glucose Cotransporter."
Weinman, E. J., Dubinsky, W. P. and Shenolikar, S., "Regulation of the Renal Na^+–H^+ Exchanger."
An excellent overview of the structure, function, and regulation of membrane transport proteins.

Seifter, J. L., and Aronson, P. S., "Properties and Physiologic Roles of the Plasma Membrane Sodium–Hydrogen Exchanger," *J. Clin. Invest.,* 78: 859–864, 1986.
An important review of the mechanism of action and role of the renal proximal tubule Na^+–H^+ exchanger.

Stone, D. K., and Xie, Xs., "Proton Translocating ATPase: Issues in Structure and Function," *Kidney Int.,* 33: 767–774, 1988.
Well-written clear explanation of the types of proton pumps and their regulation.

Weinman, E. J., Dubinsky, W., and Shenolikar, S., "Regulation of the Renal Na^+-H^+ Exchanger by Protein Phosphorylation," *Kidney Int.,* 36: 519–525, 1989.

An excellent review with more detail than the article in *Hospital Practice.*

Intracellular pH

Busa, W. B., and Nuccitelli, R., "Metabolic Regulation via Intracellular pH," *Am. J. Physiology,* 246: R409–R438, 1984.

A systematic and thorough examination of the effects of intracellular pH on cell functions.

Hoffmann, E. K., and Simonsen, L. O., "Membrane Mechanisms in Volume and pH Regulation in Vertebrate Cells," *Physiological Reviews,* 69: 315–371, 1989.

Acid–base physiology viewed from the perspective of transport physiology.

Madshus, I. H., "Regulation of Intracellular pH in Eukaryotic Cells," *Biochem. J.,* 250: 1–8, 1988.

An excellent, readable review.

Maren, T. H., "The Kinetics of HCO_3^- Synthesis Related to Fluid Secretion, pH Control, and CO_2 Elimination," *Ann. Rev. Physiol.,* 50: 695–717, 1988.

Robin, E. D., "Of Men and Mitochondria-Intracellular and Subcellular Acid–Base Relations," *N. Engl. J. Med.,* 265: 780–785, 1961.

A clear exposition of a very important concept.

Cell Signaling

Carafoli, E., and Penniston, J. T., "The Calcium Signal," *Scientific American,* 253: 70–78, 1985.

An examination of "trigger action" of calcium and the calcium-binding proteins.

Walsh, D. A., Newsholme, P., Cawley, K. C., Van Patten, S. M., and Angelos, K. L., "Motifs of Protein Phosphorylation and Mechanisms of Reversible Covalent Regulation," *Physiological Reviews,* 71(1): 285–303, 1991.

A major review of the critical role of phosphate, kinases and phosphorylases in regulating cellular activities.

Buffering

Gamble, Jr., J. L., "Evolution of Acid–Base Concept (1917–1984)," *The Physiologist,* 27(5): 375–379, 1984.

A challenging examination of what we do not understand about cellular buffering.

Renal Acid Secretion

Capasso, G., Unwin, R., Agulian, S., and Giebisch, G., "Bicarbonate Transport Along the Loop of Henle," *J. Clin. Invest.,* 88: 430–437, 1991.
Evidence that both H^+-ATPase and Na^+–H^+ exchange are involved in bicarbonate transport in this segment.

Cogan, M. G., "Regulation and Control of Bicarbonate Reabsorption in the Proximal Tubule," *Seminars in Nephrology,* 10(2): 115–121, 1990.
Review of evidence that angiotensin II plays a major role in regulating proximal tubule bicarbonate reabsorption.

Epstein, F. H., and Silva, P., "Na–K–Cl Cotransport in Chloride-Transporting Epithelia," *Annals N. Y. Academy of Sciences,* 45 : 187–197, 1985.
A comparison of the "triple transporter" in the shark rectal gland and the thick ascending limb.

Good, D. W., "Bicarbonate Absorption by the Thick Ascending Limb of Henle's Loop," *Seminars in Nephrology,* 10(2): 132–138, 1990.
A good review of the regulation of bicarbonate transport in the thick ascending limb.

Halperin, M. L., "How Much "New" Bicarbonate Is Formed in the Distal Nephron in the Process of Net Acid Excretion?" *Kidney Int.,* 35: 1277–1281, 1989.
A reexamination of "net acid excretion" in light of new insights into the transport of ammonium.

Levine, D. Z., "Single-Nephron Studies: Implications for Acid–Base Regulation," *Kidney Int.,* 38: 744–761, 1990.
An excellent review which attempts to integrate studies of acid secretion in single nephrons and nephron segments into a framework of renal acid–base disorders.

Levine, D. Z., and Jacobson, H. R., "The Regulation of Renal Acid Secretion: New Observations from Studies of Distal Nephron Segments," *Kidney Int.,* 29: 1099–1109, 1986.
An excellent review which links observations on tubular segments with whole nephron function.

Preisig, P. A., and Alpern, R. J., "Basolateral Membrane H/HCO_3 Transport in Renal Tubules," *Kidney Int.,* 39: 1077–1086, 1991.
Excellent description of mechanisms responsible for bicarbonate efflux.

Ammonia

Atkinson, D. E., and Bourke, E., "Metabolic Aspects of the Regulation of Systematic pH," *Am. J. Physiol.,* 252: F947–F956, 1987.
A highly controversial exposition of the hypothesis that hepatic ureagenesis plays a role in acid–base homeostasis.

Good, D. W., and Knepper, M. A., "Mechanisms of Ammonium Excretion: Role of the Renal Medulla," *Seminars in Nephrology,* 10(2): 166–173, 1990.
An excellent review of the transport mechanisms responsible for ammonia excretion.

Halperin, M. L., Chen, C. B., Cheema-Dhadli, S., West, M. L., and Jungas, R. L., "Is Urea Formation Regulated Primarily by Acid–Base Balance in vivo?" *Am. J. Physiol.,* 250: F605–F612, 1986.
An examination of the "Atkinson–Bourke" hypothesis.

Halperin, M. L., and Jungas, R. L., "Metabolic Production and Renal Disposal of Hydrogen Ions," *Kidney Int.,* 24: 709–713, 1983.
A quantitative assessment of the contribution of renal ammoniagenesis to renal acid secretion.

Clinical

Narins, R. G., and Emmett, M., "Simple and Mixed Acid–Base Disorders: A Practical Approach," *Medicine,* 59(3): 161–187, 1980.
Concise, thorough, well written. This is an excellent "starting point" for the understanding of clinical disorders.

Metabolic Acidosis

Arruda, J. A. L., and Kurtzman, N. A., "Mechanisms and Classification of Deranged Distal Urinary Acidification," *Am. J. Physiol.,* 239: F515–F523, 1980.
One of the "classic" papers on this subject.

DuBose, Jr., T. D., "Experimental Models of Distal Renal Tubular Acidosis," *Seminars in Nephrology,* 10(2): 174–180, 1990.
An attempt to explain distal RTA.

Madias, N. E., "Lactic Acidosis," *Kidney Int.,* 29: 752–774, 1986.
A good biochemical-physiologic review. Very good discussion of therapeutic modalities.

Metabolic Alkalosis

Berger, B. E., Cogan, M. G., and Sebastian, A., "Reduced Glomerular Filtration and Enhanced Bicarbonate Reabsorption Maintain Metabolic Alkalosis in Humans," *Kidney Int.,* 26: 205–208, 1984.
An informative study in normal subjects, illustrating the importance of reduced bicarbonate load.

Galla, J. H., and Luke, R. G., "Chloride Transport and Disorders of Acid–Base Balance," *Ann. Rev. Physiol.,* 50: 141–158, 1988.
A good review of the mechanisms responsible in chloride-responsive and chloride-resistant alkalosis.

Sabatini, S., and Kurtzman, N. A., "The Maintenance of Metabolic Alkalosis: Factors Which Decrease Bicarbonate Excretion," *Kidney Int.,* 25: 357–361, 1984.
A good review.

Respiratory Disorders

Krapf, R., Beeler, I., Hertner, D., and Hulter, H. N., "Chronic Respiratory Alkalosis—the Effect of Sustained Hyperventilation on Renal Regulation of Acid–Base Equilibrium," *N. Engl. J. Med.,* 324: 1394–1401, 1991.
An examination of the effects of hyperventilation (high altitudes) on renal acid excretion in healthy medical students.

Madias, N. E., Wolf, C. J., and Cohen, J. J., "Regulation of Acid–Base Equilibrium in Chronic Hypercapnia," *Kidney Int.,* 27: 538–543, 1985.
Under metabolic balance conditions, exposure to high CO_2 concentrations induced enhanced renal bicarbonate reabsorption in normal dogs and dogs with preexisting metabolic acidosis. The findings suggests an overriding effect on pCO_2.

Evolution

Robin, E. D., Bromberg, P. A., and Cross, C. E., "Some Aspects of the Evolution of Vertebrate Acid–Base Regulation," *Yale Journal of Biology and Medicine,* 41: 448–467, 1969.
A "must" for students of comparative acid–base physiology.

Schopf, J. W., "The Evolution of the Earliest Cells," *Scientific American,* 239:(3) 111–136, 1978.
A fascinating discussion of the metabolism of cells before the atmosphere contained oxygen.

INDEX